THE CROSS AND THE LAST WORDS

Meditations with Fulton J. Sheen

on Calvary and the Interior Life

Allan Smith

Copyright © 2025 Allan J. Smith

All rights reserved. No part of this book may be reproduced in any form without written permission from the publisher, except brief quotations used in reviews or articles.

Scripture quotations in this book are taken from the Revised Standard Version – Catholic Edition, Second Edition (RSV-2CE).

Archbishop Fulton J. Sheen himself often quoted from the Douay-Rheims Bible; this edition uses the RSV-2CE for clarity while preserving the devotional tone of his insights.

Excerpts from the works of Archbishop Fulton J. Sheen are used with permission where applicable.

Published by: Bishop Sheen Today

www.bishopsheentoday.com

Title: The Cross and the Last Words. Meditations with Fulton J. Sheen on Calvary and the Interior Life.

Compiled by Allan J. Smith. Includes bibliographical references.

Book formatting and design by Ajayi Isaac details
mailto:smeplegacy@gmail.com/ +2348162435897

Identifiers:

Paperback: 978-1-997627-72-2

eBook: 978-1-997627-73-9

Hardcover: 978-1-997627-74-6

Subjects: Jesus Christ — The Blessed Virgin Mary — Prayer and Meditation – The Holy Face Devotion - St. Thérèse of Lisieux – Archbishop Fulton J. Sheen – Lives of the Saints – The Cross – The Seven Last Words

THE CROSS AND THE LAST WORDS

Meditations with Fulton J. Sheen on Calvary and the Interior Life

A Sheen Mission Series – Volume III

The Sheen Mission Series invites you to walk with Archbishop Fulton J. Sheen in prayer, reparation, and renewal – a journey of the Holy Face, the Cross, the Eucharist, and Our Blessed Mother.

Description:

The Cross and the Last Words is the third volume in the Sheen Mission Series – a treasury of meditations on Calvary and the Seven Last Words of Christ.

Archbishop Fulton Sheen, known worldwide for his preaching on the Cross, offers profound insights into forgiveness, mercy, suffering, and hope. This volume invites you to stand at the foot of the Cross, to hear again the words of the dying Christ, and to discover their power to heal and renew your life.

Series Note:

This book is the third of four volumes in *The Sheen Mission Series*, a collection of spiritual companions for personal devotion and parish renewal:

1. **Volume I - *The Holy Face and the Little Way***
2. **Volume II - *Behold Your Mother***
3. **Volume IV - *Lord, Show Us Thy Face and We Shall Be Saved***

"Calvary is the mountain where all the love of God is revealed. In the Seven Last Words, we hear the heart of Christ speaking to the heart of the world."

— Archbishop Fulton J. Sheen

Dedication:

**To Our Lady
of the Holy Name of God**

&

**To all who kneel
at the foot of the Cross,
seeking mercy, healing,
and the love that saves.**

J M J

Archbishop Fulton J. Sheen, known throughout the world for his preaching on the Cross, provided us over the years with many powerful meditations on Christ's Passion and His Seven Last Words. As a Scripture scholar, he understood the transforming power of preaching Christ crucified. With St. Paul, he could affirm: *"For I am determined to know nothing among you except Jesus Christ, and Him crucified."* (1 Corinthians 2:2)

In his final Good Friday address in 1979, Archbishop Sheen reflected that he had offered meditations on the Seven Last Words "for fifty-eight years." From his earliest days as a young priest in Peoria, Illinois, to his years as a university professor in Washington, DC and later as a bishop in New York, his words left an indelible mark on countless souls.

Recognizing their timeless importance, this third volume in the *Sheen Mission Series* gathers some of his most treasured insights on Calvary and the interior life. In addition to these reflections, readers will also find traditional Catholic prayers that have inspired countless souls.

In helping the reader to apply the Seven Last Words of Christ into their daily lives, Archbishop Sheen demonstrates how it is possible to practice virtue, renounce vice, and live the Beatitudes — all illuminated by the saving words of Christ from the Cross.

It is my prayer that these meditations will draw the reader to the foot of Calvary, where Our Blessed Lord still speaks to us today.

Archbishop Sheen once reminded us that "books are the most patient of teachers." May this book prove to be such a teacher, a faithful companion on your journey to healing, hope, and renewal of your life in Christ.

Sit Nomen Domini Benedictum!

Blessed be the Name of the Lord!

Allan J. Smith

September 14, 2025

Feast of the Exaltation of the Cross

Table of Contents

J M J xi

Epigraph xxiii

Foreword 1

Introduction: Why the Cross? Why Now? 3

Chapter 1: The Cross and the Mystery of Suffering ... 6

Chapter 2: The Cross as the School of Love 9

Chapter 3: The First Word "Father, Forgive Them" . 12

Chapter 4: The Second Word: "This Day You Will Be with Me in Paradise" 15

Chapter 5: The Third Word "Behold Your Mother" . 18

Chapter 6: The Fourth Word: "My God, My God" ... 21

Chapter 7: The Fifth Word: "I Thirst" 24

Chapter 8: The Sixth Word: "It Is Finished" 27

Chapter 9: The Seventh Word: "Father, Into Your Hands I Commit My Spirit" 30

Chapter 10: Calvary in Daily Life 33

Chapter 11: Healing at the Foot of the Cross 36

Chapter 12: Living in the Shadow of the Cross 39

Chapter 13: The Power of the Resurrection through the Cross 42

Chapter 14: The Cross and the Eucharist 45

Chapter 15: The Cross and Eternal Life 48

Chapter 16: The Cross and Christian Discipleship ... 51

xv

Chapter 17: The Cross and the Beatitudes.................. 54

Chapter 18: The Cross and the Church....................... 57

Chapter 19: The Cross and the Priesthood................. 60

Chapter 20: The Cross and Reparation 63

Chapter 21: The Cross and Hope................................ 66

Chapter 22: The Cross and Love.................................. 69

Chapter 23: The Cross and the Christian Life............ 72

Chapter 24: The Cross and the Saints......................... 75

Chapter 25: The Cross and Eternal Glory................... 78

Chapter 26: The Cross and Our Daily Mission.......... 81

Chapter 27: The Cross and Victory.............................. 84

Chapter 28: The Cross and Peace................................. 87

Chapter 29: The Cross and Joy 90

Chapter 30: The Cross and the Christian Home........ 93

Chapter 31: The Cross and the World......................... 96

Chapter 32: The Cross and the Christian Apostolate 99

Chapter 33: The Cross and the Mystical Body.......... 102

Chapter 34: The Cross and the Sacraments............... 105

Chapter 35: The Cross and Mary 108

Chapter 36: The Cross and the Mass.......................... 111

Chapter 37: The Cross and Christian Virtue 114

Chapter 38: The Cross and the Christian Nation 117

Chapter 39: The Cross and Perseverance 120

Chapter 40: The Cross and Final Perseverance 123

Chapter 41: The Cross and Eternal Salvation 126

Chapter 42: The Cross and Eternity 129

Chapter 43: Conclusion: The Cross and the Christian Soul 132

Epilogue: Living the Fruits of the Cross 135

Note on the Appendices 139

Appendix I: Fulton Sheen on the Seven Last Words 141

   On the First Word – "Father, Forgive Them" 141

   On the Second Word – "This Day You Will Be with Me in Paradise" 142

   On the Third Word – "Behold Your Mother" 142

   On the Fourth Word – "My God, My God, Why Have You Forsaken Me?" 143

   On the Fifth Word – "I Thirst" 143

   On the Sixth Word – "It Is Finished" 144

   On the Seventh Word – "Father, Into Your Hands I Commit My Spirit" 144

Appendix II: Prayers Before the Crucifix 145

   The Anima Christi 145

   Sheen's Meditation Before the Cross 147

Prayer of Surrender at Calvary *(Inspired by the Seventh Word)* 148

Appendix III: Stations of the Cross 149
    Stations of the Cross 153

Appendix IV: Suggested Scriptures 157
    Prophecies of the Passion *(Old Testament)* 158
    The Last Supper and Gethsemane 159
    The Trial and Condemnation 159
    The Way of the Cross 160
    The Seven Last Words *(Gospel References)* 160
    Death and Burial of Jesus 161

Appendix V: Hymns and Chants of the Passion 163
    Stabat Mater Dolorosa 163
    Pange Lingua Gloriosi *(English)* 168
    Liturgical Note 170

Appendix VI: Guide to Making a Holy Hour at Calvary 171
    Guide to Making a Holy Hour at Calvary 174

Appendix VII: Overcoming Sin, Practicing Virtue and Living the Beatitudes 177

    Introduction 177

    Overcoming Sin 178

    Practicing Virtue 178

    Living the Beatitudes 180

Conclusion 182

Introduction to Reflections on Practicing Virtue, Overcoming Sin, and Living the Beatitudes 183

Part I Overcoming Sin 185

    Introduction 185

    Reflection 1: Overcoming the Sin of Anger 186

    Reflection 2: Overcoming the Sin of Envy 189

    Reflection 3: Overcoming the Sin of Lust 192

    Reflection 4: Overcoming the Sin of Pride 195

    Reflection 5: Overcoming the Sin of Gluttony 198

    Reflection 6: Overcoming the Sin of Sloth 201

    Reflection 7: Overcoming the Sin of Greed 204

Part II – Practicing Virtue 207

    Introduction 207

    Reflection 1: Practicing the Virtue of Fortitude ... 208

    Reflection 2: Practicing the Virtue of Hope 211

Reflection 3: Practicing the Virtue of Prudence .. 214

Reflection 4: Practicing the Virtue of Faith 217

Reflection 5: Practicing the Virtue of Temperance 220

Reflection 6: Practicing the Virtue of Justice 223

Reflection 7: Practicing the Virtue of Charity 226

Part III – Living the Beatitudes 229

Introduction 229

Reflection 1: Living the Beatitude: Blessed are the meek, for they shall inherit the earth. 231

Reflection 2: Living the Beatitude: Blessed are the merciful, for they shall obtain mercy. 234

Reflection 3: Living the Beatitude: Blessed are the pure in heart, for they shall see God. 237

Reflection 4 Living the Beatitude: Blessed are the poor in spirit, for theirs is the kingdom of heaven. 240

Reflection 5: Living the Beatitude: Blessed are those who hunger and thirst for justice, for they shall be satisfied. 243

Reflection 6: Living the Beatitude: Blessed are the peacemakers, for they shall be called children of God. 246

Reflection 7: Living the Beatitude: Blessed are those who mourn, for they shall be comforted. 249

Reflection 8: Living the Beatitude: Blessed are those who are persecuted for righteousness' sake, for theirs is the kingdom of heaven. 252

Epilogue: The Cross and the Christian Way of Life 255

Concluding Word: Sent from Calvary 256

About the Author 258

About the Sheen Mission Series 260

J M J 261

Epigraph

"When they came to the place which is called The Skull, there they crucified him, and the criminals, one on the right and one on the left. And Jesus said, 'Father, forgive them; for they know not what they do.' ... Then Jesus, crying with a loud voice, said, 'Father, into thy hands I commit my spirit!' And having said this he breathed his last."

Luke 23:33–46

"The Cross is not merely an incident in the life of Our Lord; it is the mission pulpit from which He preaches to the world His most eloquent sermon — the sermon of redeeming love."

Archbishop Fulton J. Sheen
(The Seven Last Words)

Foreword

The Cross is the pulpit from which Christ preached His greatest sermon. Each word spoken from Calvary was not only addressed to those gathered beneath the wood, but to every soul across time who would dare to listen.

Archbishop Fulton J. Sheen made it his life's mission to help the world listen again. For fifty-eight consecutive Good Fridays, he offered meditations on the Seven Last Words of Jesus. His voice echoed across cathedrals, airwaves, and television screens, reminding the faithful that these words are not relics of the past but living streams of mercy for the present.

Why do we return to the Cross? Because in a world wounded by sin, suffering, and division, the last words of Christ reveal a medicine stronger than our wounds. They unveil the depth of divine love, the gravity of human sin, and the triumph of mercy over despair.

This book is not simply a collection of meditations; it is a pilgrimage. Each reflection invites you to kneel at the foot of Calvary, to hear anew the words of the dying Christ, and to let them heal and renew your heart.

Archbishop Sheen often said, "Unless there is a Good Friday in your life, there can be no Easter Sunday." May these pages help you embrace the Cross, not as a symbol of sorrow alone, but as the surest path to resurrection.

Introduction:
Why the Cross? Why Now?

Every age has its question, its trial, its wound. For our time, it is the flight from suffering. We run from the Cross in search of comfort, distraction, or control — and yet in doing so, we run from the very place where love is revealed.

Why the Cross? Because it is here that human sin and divine mercy meet. It is here that the ugliness of hatred is overcome by the beauty of sacrifice. It is here that we see, not in theory but in flesh and blood, what love truly means. The Cross is not an accessory to Christianity; it is its center. Without it, our faith becomes sentiment. With it, our faith becomes salvation.

Archbishop Fulton J. Sheen once said, *"The Cross is the only ladder high enough to touch Heaven."* To gaze upon it is to discover the measure of God's love and the seriousness of our sin. To embrace it is to find not defeat but redemption, not sorrow but joy, not death but life.

Why now? Because the world has never been more in need of meaning. We suffer — in body, in mind, in spirit — and yet so often without purpose. The Cross gives purpose. It tells us that pain is not wasted, that wounds can be healed, and that sacrifice can redeem. It transforms tragedy into triumph and sorrow into song.

Archbishop Fulton Sheen once observed that Calvary is the place where the drama of human sin and divine mercy meet. It is here that we discover the meaning of our own trials, for the Cross is not simply the story of what Christ endured — it is the key to what we are called to become.

In an age that seeks to escape suffering, Christ invites us to enter it with Him. He does not promise a life without crosses; He promises that no cross will be without Him. And in that promise, we find hope.

This volume is an invitation to stand with Mary, with John, and with the repentant thief — to hear again the words of Jesus from the Cross and to let them shape our hearts. Each meditation is a call to reparation, to surrender, to trust. Each word is a gift.

Let us then take up the ancient prayer of the Church: *"We adore You, O Christ, and we bless You, because by Your Holy Cross You have redeemed the world."*

Chapter 1: The Cross and the Mystery of Suffering

Reflection – The Core Lesson of Suffering

Suffering is not an elective in the school of life — it is a required course. For some, it arrives like a sudden storm; for others, it lingers like a long shadow. Our first instinct is often escape. But the Cross teaches us to ask a different question: *Who suffers with me?*

Archbishop Fulton Sheen reminded us that Calvary is the only classroom where pain finds meaning. "When we suffer without Christ," he said, "we suffer alone; when we suffer with Christ, we share in the work of redemption."

Sheen on Redemptive Suffering

"In the modern world, there is much concern for eliminating suffering, but little understanding of its place in the plan of God. Our Lord did not come to remove the Cross from life, but to lift life

into the Cross, making it redemptive. By uniting our wounds to His, we discover that pain can be fruitful, love can be purified, and hope can be born from ashes."

Sheen saw suffering not as an interruption to God's plan but as an instrument of it. The nails did not hold Christ to the Cross — love did. And that same love can hold us steady when our own trials press hard.

Illustration – A Mother's Loss

There is the story of a mother who, after losing her child, chose to offer her grief to parents who had never known faith. She could not undo her loss, but she could decide what her loss would mean. Like the Blessed Mother at Calvary, she stood in the place where pain and faith meet — and chose to believe that the Cross is never the end.

Her witness became light to others in darkness. Through her tears, she revealed the same truth the Cross reveals: suffering, when united to Christ, becomes a channel of mercy.

Invitation – Choosing the Meaning of Our Cross

If suffering is inevitable, we must decide whether it will be wasted or offered. Christ's Cross teaches us to "waste nothing" — not a tear, not a sleepless night, not a hidden wound. Every trial can become a prayer, every sorrow a seed of compassion.

Stand at Calvary with Mary and John. Look upon the Crucified and ask:

- *What Cross am I carrying right now?*
- *Am I carrying it alone, or with Him?*

When we surrender our suffering to the Cross, it ceases to be only ours. It becomes His — and in Him, it becomes redemptive.

Closing Prayer

Lord Jesus, You carried the weight of the world's sin upon Your shoulders. Teach me to unite my sorrows to Yours, so that nothing in my life may be wasted. May every wound become a window for Your grace, every trial an offering of love. Keep me at the foot of Your Cross, where suffering is no longer meaningless but fruitful in Your mercy. **Amen.**

Chapter 2:
The Cross as the School of Love

Reflection – Learning Love at Calvary

Every human heart longs to love and be loved, yet our understanding of love is often shallow. We mistake it for sentiment, possession, or passing desire. The Cross reveals something different: love that is sacrificial, steadfast, and willing to suffer for the beloved.

On Calvary, Jesus does not merely speak of love — He demonstrates it. His arms, stretched wide upon the wood, become the open classroom where we learn that true love always costs something.

Sheen on Love's Lesson

"Love is not measured by how much it receives, but by how much it gives. The Cross is not only the proof of Christ's love for us; it is the pattern of what our love must be for others. Love that refuses sacrifice is not love at all."

Archbishop Sheen insisted that Calvary is the "school of love," where every disciple must sit and learn. In a world that prizes comfort and convenience, the Cross teaches that love is forged in fire, not in ease.

Illustration – A Hidden Sacrifice

A priest once shared the story of an elderly parishioner who, after years of caring for her disabled husband, whispered: *"I thought I was keeping him alive, but he was teaching me how to love."*

Her daily acts — spoon-feeding, lifting, bathing, praying beside his bed — were hidden from the world, but radiant before God. Like Mary at the foot of the Cross, she discovered that love is not defined by ease but by endurance.

Invitation – Enrolling in Love's School

The Cross is not an optional course in the Christian life; it is the very curriculum. Every wound we bear, every burden we carry, becomes a lesson in love when united to Christ.

Ask yourself:

- *Where am I being invited to love beyond comfort?*
- *Who in my life needs not just my affection, but my sacrifice?*
- *Am I willing to let the Cross teach me love — even when it hurts?*

To sit at the foot of the Cross is to let Jesus Himself tutor us in the ways of self-giving.

Closing Prayer

Crucified Lord, Teacher of Love, show me that true love is more than words — it is sacrifice. Give me patience when I grow weary, generosity when I want to withdraw, and courage when love demands a Cross. May Your school of Calvary shape my heart, until it beats in union with Yours.

Amen.

Chapter 3:
The First Word
"Father, Forgive Them"

Reflection – The Scandal of Forgiveness

The first word from the Cross is not a cry of protest, but a prayer of mercy. In the face of betrayal, injustice, and cruelty, Jesus does not condemn His executioners. He asks the Father to forgive them.

This moment unveils the heart of God: mercy poured out where vengeance might have been expected. At Calvary, forgiveness is no longer an idea — it becomes flesh and blood.

Sheen on Mercy at the Cross

"The world expected anger, but Christ gave pardon. The Cross is not only the pulpit of pain, it is the pulpit of forgiveness. If we are to be His disciples, then we must forgive — not seven times, but seventy times seven."

Archbishop Sheen taught that Christ's first word shatters the cycle of hatred. He reveals that evil is not overcome by more evil, but by love that refuses retaliation.

Illustration – A Prisoner's Conversion

A chaplain once recounted the story of a man imprisoned for violence, whose heart was hardened by years of bitterness. One day, reading the words of Jesus on the Cross — *"Father, forgive them"* — he realized he had never forgiven those who had hurt him, nor sought forgiveness for his own crimes.

That encounter became the turning point of his life. He began to pray daily for his victims and for the grace to forgive. Slowly, the chains around his soul were loosed. Mercy set him free long before the prison gates ever would.

Invitation – Living the First Word

The hardest words to say are often the simplest: *"I forgive you."* Yet without them, peace remains impossible. The Cross shows us that forgiveness is not weakness but strength — the strength to love as God loves.

Ask yourself:

- *Who do I still hold in the prison of my resentment?*
- *Where is Christ inviting me to break the cycle of anger?*
- *Am I willing to pray, even through tears, "Father, forgive them" for those who have wounded me?*

Closing Prayer

Merciful Jesus, Your first word from the Cross was forgiveness. Teach me to forgive as You forgive — freely, fully, and without condition. Heal the wounds in my heart that resist mercy. Let my life echo Your prayer, until every bitterness is consumed in Your love.

Amen.

Chapter 4:
The Second Word:
"This Day You Will Be with Me in Paradise"

Reflection – The Promise of Mercy

Beside Christ hung two criminals. One cursed, the other confessed. One turned inward in despair, the other outward in hope. To the repentant thief, Jesus spoke a word more precious than freedom: *"This day you will be with Me in Paradise."*

This second word reveals the immediacy of grace. Heaven is not a reward for the perfect, but a gift for the repentant. In a single act of trust — *"Jesus, remember me"* — a sinner gained eternity.

Sheen on the Good Thief

"The thief on the right had no good works to his credit, no reputation to uphold, no promises he could keep. He had only a heart that could trust.

And that was enough. In one instant, a lifetime of sin was swallowed up by a moment of faith."

Archbishop Sheen loved to point out that the thief stole heaven in the final hour. He is the patron saint of hope for every soul who fears it is too late.

Illustration – A Deathbed Grace

A priest once recalled being called to the bedside of a man who had not entered a church in over fifty years. With tears, the man whispered: *"Father, is it too late for me?"* The priest placed the crucifix in his hands and repeated the words of Christ to the thief: *"This day you will be with Me in Paradise."*

That dying man, like the good thief, found peace in surrender. His last breath was not a sigh of despair, but of hope — proof that God's mercy never comes too late.

Invitation – Trusting the Promise

The thief's prayer is short, simple, and unforgettable: *"Jesus, remember me."* It is a prayer anyone can pray, in joy or sorrow, in strength or weakness. It is the prayer of a child returning home.

Ask yourself:

- *Do I believe God's mercy can reach even the darkest corners of my life?*
- *Am I willing to entrust my future – and my eternity – to His promise?*
- *Who in my life needs to hear the hope that it is never too late to turn back to God?*

Closing Prayer

Jesus, Savior of the lost, remember me when my strength fails and my heart falters. Remember me in my weakness, and bring me into the light of Your Kingdom. Let my last words echo the prayer of the good thief: *"Jesus, remember me."*

Amen.

Chapter 5:
The Third Word
"Behold Your Mother"

Reflection – A Gift from the Cross

At Calvary, Jesus looked down and saw His Mother and the beloved disciple. With His strength waning, He entrusted them to each other: *"Woman, behold your son … Behold your mother."*

This third word is not only about Mary and John. It is about us. In His final moments, Christ gave His Mother to every believer. At the foot of the Cross, we received not only forgiveness but family.

Sheen on Mary's Mission

"Mary is not just a memory in the drama of Calvary. She is the Mother whom Christ gave to us that we might never again be orphans. At the foot of the Cross, she became the Mother of all who would be reborn in grace."

Archbishop Sheen taught that Christ, by giving us His Mother, gave us the perfect companion for the journey of faith. She consoles, intercedes, and teaches us how to remain at the Cross when others flee.

Illustration – A Soldier's Consolation

A young soldier, gravely wounded, was once asked in his last hours what brought him peace. He pointed to a medal of the Blessed Virgin around his neck and whispered: *"She is my Mother. I am not afraid."*

Like John, he discovered that in Mary's presence, we are never alone. Her maternal love draws us closer to Jesus and strengthens us to endure our own crosses.

Invitation – Receiving Our Mother

Jesus' gift of Mary is not symbolic. It is real, personal, and enduring. Each of us is invited to take her into our homes, into our hearts, and into our daily prayer.

Ask yourself:

- *Have I truly welcomed Mary as my Mother, or kept her at a distance?*
- *Do I bring my struggles to her, as a child brings them to a parent?*
- *How can I imitate John by making space for her in my life today?*

Closing Prayer

Mary, Mother of Jesus and my Mother, teach me to stand faithfully at the Cross. Comfort me in sorrow, strengthen me in trial, and lead me always to your Son. May I never forget that you are near, and that in your embrace I am never alone.

Amen.

Chapter 6:
The Fourth Word: "My God, My God, Why Have You Forsaken Me?"

Reflection – The Cry of Abandonment

At the height of His agony, Jesus cried out the words of Psalm 22: *"My God, my God, why have You forsaken Me?"* This is perhaps the most haunting of the Seven Last Words. It reveals not only the depth of His suffering but also the depth of His love — for He chose to enter even into the experience of seeming abandonment.

This cry is not despair, but prayer. In uttering the Psalm, Jesus shows us that even in the darkest night, the soul can cling to God.

Sheen on the Mystery of Forsakenness

"There is no suffering in the world which He did not make His own. In crying out to the Father, He gave a voice to every lonely soul, every broken heart, every abandoned child. He was not forsaken so that we might never be."

Archbishop Sheen explained that Christ bore the silence of God so that we would never have to face it alone. What seems to be absence is, in truth, the most profound nearness.

Illustration – A Silent Night of Faith

A religious sister once endured years of spiritual dryness, feeling that God had hidden His face from her. She later confided: *"In that silence, I learned to love Him without consolation. I discovered that faith is not about feelings but about fidelity."*

Her hidden trial reflected the mystery of Christ's cry — that love endures even when heaven seems silent.

Invitation – Praying Through the Silence

Every Christian, at some point, feels the shadow of abandonment: unanswered prayers, losses, loneliness. Christ has already stood there, sanctifying that place with His presence.

Ask yourself:

- *When have I felt abandoned by God?*
- *Can I unite that pain with Christ's cry on the Cross?*
- *Am I willing to keep praying, even when God seems silent?*

Closing Prayer

Jesus, who cried to the Father in the hour of darkness, be with me when I feel forsaken. Teach me to trust that even in silence, the Father's love is near. May my own cry of pain become a prayer of faith, until it is answered in the light of Your Resurrection.

Amen.

Chapter 7:
The Fifth Word: "I Thirst"

Reflection – The Cry of Desire

After hours of agony, Jesus spoke two simple words: *"I thirst."* On one level, it was the physical thirst of a body drained of blood and strength. But beneath it lies a deeper truth: the thirst of God for souls.

The Cross reveals that Christ's longing is not for water alone, but for love — your love, my love, the love of every human heart. His thirst is the eternal desire that none be lost.

Sheen on the Thirst of Christ

"When He said, 'I thirst,' He was not only asking for water. He was thirsting for souls, thirsting for our love, thirsting for the return of the creatures He came to redeem. His thirst still remains — for until the last soul is saved, His Heart is not satisfied."

Archbishop Sheen reminded us that the thirst of Christ is ongoing. He thirsts not only from the Cross, but in every tabernacle, every altar, every soul that still wanders far from Him.

Illustration – The Missionary's Encounter

A missionary once shared how he preached about Christ's thirst in a remote village. A young woman approached afterward and said: *"I never knew God desired me. I thought I was the one chasing Him. Now I see that He has been thirsting for me all along."*

Her discovery changed her life. She entered the Church, not out of fear, but out of the joy of being wanted by God.

Invitation – Quenching His Thirst

Jesus' cry is a call to each of us. He thirsts for our faith, our love, our surrender. And He thirsts through the needs of others — the poor, the lonely, the forgotten. To love them is to give Him drink.

Ask yourself:

- *Do I believe that Jesus truly thirsts for me personally?*
- *How can I offer Him the drink of my love today?*
- *Where is He thirsting in the suffering of others around me?*

Closing Prayer

O Jesus, burning with thirst upon the Cross, quench Your longing in my poor love. Take my heart as Your refreshment, my prayers as Your drink, my acts of charity as Your consolation. May I never forget that You thirst for me, and may I thirst only for You.

Amen.

Chapter 8:
The Sixth Word: "It Is Finished"

Reflection – The Triumph of Completion

As His final moments approached, Jesus proclaimed: *"It is finished."* These words are not a sigh of defeat but a declaration of victory. The work the Father had given Him — the work of redemption — was now complete.

The Cross reveals that love does not stop halfway. Christ embraced every suffering, every humiliation, every drop of the chalice of sacrifice. Nothing was left undone.

Sheen on the Fulfillment of the Cross

"When Our Lord said, 'It is finished,' He was not saying, 'It is over.' He was saying, 'It is accomplished.' The world's salvation was won, the debt was paid, the sacrifice complete. No task was left unfulfilled, no suffering wasted."

Archbishop Sheen taught that these words remind us that true love perseveres to the end. Our vocations, our duties, our crosses are not measured by beginnings alone, but by fidelity to completion.

Illustration – A Life Faithfully Lived

A nun who had served in hidden poverty for fifty years was once asked what gave her strength. She answered simply: *"I just wanted to finish what God gave me to do."*

Her life bore no fame, no worldly reward. Yet in her quiet perseverance, she mirrored the words of Christ: *"It is finished."* Love had been carried through to the end.

Invitation – Persevering in Love

The sixth word invites us to reflect on our own commitments — to God, to family, to vocation. Do we carry them only when easy, or do we persevere to completion?

Ask yourself:

- *What mission or duty has God entrusted to me that I am tempted to leave unfinished?*
- *Can I offer my daily sacrifices as part of Christ's completed work of love?*
- *Am I willing to remain faithful to the end, trusting that nothing offered in love is wasted?*

Closing Prayer

Lord Jesus, who finished the work the Father gave You, strengthen me to persevere in the tasks entrusted to me. When I grow weary, remind me of Your Cross. When I am tempted to quit, remind me of Your love. Let me one day echo Your words with peace: *"It is finished."*

Amen.

Chapter 9:
The Seventh Word:
"Father, Into Your Hands I Commit My Spirit"

Reflection – The Surrender of the Son

The final word of Jesus is a prayer of trust: *"Father, into Your hands I commit My spirit."* After the agony, after the darkness, after the silence, He rests everything in the Father's embrace.

This is the summit of the Cross — surrender. The One who came from the Father now returns to Him, teaching us that the end of every life, if lived in faith, is not despair but homecoming.

Sheen on the Peace of Surrender

"Our Lord died as He lived: offering Himself in perfect obedience to the Father. The Cross was not taken from Him; it was freely given. In surrendering His spirit, He shows us that the last act of life is not to cling, but to commend."

Archbishop Sheen reminded us that death, in Christ, is no longer the great terror. It has become the final act of love — a placing of our lives back into the Father's hands.

Illustration – A Childlike Trust

A saintly priest was once asked what he feared most about dying. He replied: *"Nothing. For I know whose hands will catch me when I fall."*

His answer reflects the heart of Christ's final word: trust as simple and complete as that of a child leaping into a father's arms.

Invitation – Learning to Let Go

Every day offers opportunities to practice this surrender: letting go of control, of fear, of our own will. In small deaths — of pride, of resentment, of selfishness — we prepare for that final surrender into the Father's hands.

Ask yourself:

- *What am I still clinging to that I need to entrust to God?*
- *Can I make of my life a daily act of surrender, echoing Jesus' final word?*
- *Do I live with the confidence that my true home is with the Father?*

Closing Prayer

Father, into Your hands I commend my spirit. Take what I fear to surrender, hold what I cannot carry, and receive what I cannot keep. At the hour of my death, may I rest in Your embrace, with the peace of Christ upon my lips.

Amen.

Chapter 10:
Calvary in Daily Life

Reflection – The Cross Beyond Good Friday

Calvary is not only a hill outside Jerusalem; it is the pattern of every Christian life. Each day offers a share in Christ's sacrifice — in small annoyances, hidden sacrifices, quiet sufferings, and moments of fidelity.

To live the Christian life is to carry the Cross not only in church, but at home, at work, in family struggles, in disappointments, and even in the silence of unanswered prayers. Calvary continues wherever love meets suffering.

Sheen on Everyday Crosses

"There is no escaping the Cross. We can either drag it, cursing the weight, or we can embrace it, finding in it the seed of redemption. The difference is not in the Cross itself, but in the spirit with which we carry it."

Archbishop Sheen insisted that our daily trials, united with Christ, become channels of grace. When borne with love, even the smallest crosses can sanctify the soul and bless the world.

Illustration – The Hidden Heroism of the Ordinary

A father rises early to provide for his family, enduring long hours with patience. A mother silently offers her exhaustion in caring for her children. A sick parishioner unites his suffering to the Lord for the salvation of souls.

None of these acts will be recorded in history books, but in heaven, they shine brighter than gold. They are Calvary lived in ordinary life.

Invitation – Embracing Daily Crosses

Each day we face a choice: to resent our burdens or to offer them. In the school of the Cross, nothing is wasted when placed in Christ's hands.

Ask yourself:

- *What small cross can I carry with love today?*
- *Do I see the hidden sufferings of my life as obstacles, or as opportunities for grace?*
- *Am I willing to let my daily life become a continuation of Calvary?*

Closing Prayer

Lord Jesus, teach me to find Calvary in the ordinary moments of my life. Help me embrace my daily crosses, not with bitterness, but with love. May every sacrifice, however small, be joined to Yours, until my whole life becomes an offering upon the altar of Your Cross.

Amen.

Chapter 11:
Healing at the Foot of the Cross

Reflection – Where Wounds Meet Mercy

At the foot of the Cross, the broken find their healing. Mary, John, and the faithful few stood near Jesus as His blood and water flowed forth — streams of mercy for the wounded world.

The Cross is not only a place of suffering but also a fountain of grace. To kneel at Calvary is to discover that our wounds are not the end; they can become the place where God's mercy enters.

Sheen on the Cross as Medicine

"The Cross is the hospital of souls. It is there we learn that our sickness is sin, and our remedy is grace. No wound is too deep, no scar too lasting, that it cannot be healed by the pierced Heart of Christ."

Archbishop Sheen often spoke of the Cross as both diagnosis and cure — it reveals the gravity of sin, but also the greater power of redemption.

Illustration – A Pilgrim's Peace

A pilgrim once entered a chapel of the Crucifixion, carrying years of resentment and guilt. As she gazed at the crucified Lord, her tears fell like rain. Later she testified: *"For the first time, I felt forgiven. My wounds were still there, but they were no longer poisoned. They were touched by His wounds."*

Her experience reflects what countless souls discover: healing begins not by running from the Cross but by standing beneath it.

Invitation – Bringing Our Wounds to the Cross

Every heart carries scars: from sin, betrayal, illness, or loss. Calvary invites us to place those wounds into the wounded hands of Christ. Only there do they become transformed.

Ask yourself:

- *What wound in my life most needs the healing touch of Christ?*
- *Am I willing to let His mercy flow into that pain, even if it means reopening it in prayer?*
- *How can I be a source of healing for others by leading them to the Cross?*

Closing Prayer

Jesus, Divine Physician, I bring You the wounds of my heart. Touch them with Your pierced hands, cleanse them with the water and blood from Your side, and make of them channels of compassion for others. At the foot of Your Cross, may I find not despair but healing, not death but new life.

Amen.

Chapter 12:
Living in the Shadow of the Cross

Reflection – The Cross as Our Daily Companion

The Cross is not only an event of the past; it casts its shadow across every age and every soul. To live in its shadow is not to live in despair, but to live in the constant reminder of God's love poured out for us.

The shadow of the Cross follows us in our trials, in our choices, and in our prayer. It reminds us that there is no suffering Christ has not shared, no darkness He has not entered, and no burden He will not help us carry.

Sheen on the Ever-Present Cross

"Calvary is not just a place; it is a condition. We do not escape the Cross by avoiding it, but by carrying it with Christ. The Christian never leaves Calvary – he carries its shadow with him wherever he goes."

Archbishop Sheen explained that the Cross is the Christian's constant companion. It teaches us how to live, how to love, and even how to die — always in union with the One who bore it first.

Illustration – A Hidden Witness

A layman once testified that for years he kept a small crucifix in his pocket. Whenever he felt tempted, discouraged, or lonely, he would hold it tightly and whisper: *"I am not alone. He is with me."*

That simple practice became his way of living in the shadow of the Cross — not as a burden, but as a source of strength.

Invitation – Embracing the Shadow

To live in the shadow of the Cross is to let every part of our life be touched by Calvary. Our joys and sorrows, our work and rest, our prayers and relationships — all can be sanctified when brought beneath its shadow.

Ask yourself:

- *Do I see the Cross as something far away, or as a daily presence in my life?*
- *How can I let the remembrance of the Cross shape my choices today?*
- *Am I willing to let its shadow fall on my life, not as darkness, but as light?*

Closing Prayer

Lord Jesus, keep me always in the shadow of Your Cross. When I am tempted, remind me of Your victory. When I am weary, remind me of Your love. When I am joyful, remind me of Your sacrifice. May every step I take be illumined by the shadow that saves.

Amen.

Chapter 13:
The Power of the Resurrection through the Cross

Reflection – The Light Beyond the Darkness

The Cross and the Resurrection are inseparable. Calvary was not the end; it was the doorway to Easter morning. By embracing the Cross, Jesus transformed it into the very path of glory.

For the Christian, this means that every suffering united with Christ carries within it a seed of resurrection. Death is not the final word. Love is.

Sheen on the Triumph of the Cross

"The world thinks of the Cross as failure. But without Good Friday, there would be no Easter. Christ has turned the Cross from a symbol of defeat into the very condition of victory. In every Christian life, the Cross is the prelude to resurrection."

Archbishop Sheen taught that the Resurrection does not cancel the Cross, but crowns it. The wounds remain, but they shine with glory.

Illustration – Hope after Loss

A widow once reflected that after her husband's death, she felt buried in grief. But slowly, as she united her sorrow to Christ, she began to see signs of new life: deeper prayer, compassion for others, and an unshakable hope in eternal reunion.

Her testimony echoed Easter morning — the dawn that rises only after the long night of Good Friday.

Invitation – Living the Paschal Mystery

Every trial we endure can become a share in the Paschal Mystery — Cross and Resurrection. To embrace the Cross is to trust that new life will follow, though unseen for now.

Ask yourself:

- *Where do I need to believe that God can bring resurrection from my suffering?*
- *Do I live with the hope that no cross is final?*
- *Am I willing to let Christ's victory be my confidence, even in dark hours?*

Closing Prayer

Risen Lord, You turned the Cross into victory and death into life. Teach me to see my trials as seeds of resurrection. Fill me with hope that no suffering is wasted, and that Easter always follows Good Friday. May I live in the joy of Your triumph, and share it with all I meet.

Amen.

Chapter 14:
The Cross and the Eucharist

Reflection – Calvary Made Present

At the Last Supper, Jesus gave His disciples bread and wine, saying: *"This is My Body ... This is My Blood."* On Calvary, He fulfilled that gift with His sacrifice. The Eucharist is not a memory of the Cross but its living presence.

Every Mass is Calvary renewed — the same Body broken, the same Blood poured out, offered now for us in sacramental form. To approach the Eucharist is to stand at the foot of the Cross and receive its grace.

Sheen on the Eucharistic Sacrifice

"The Mass is the re-presentation of Calvary. The difference is that on Calvary Christ was alone; in the Mass, He invites us to join Him. The Cross is lifted out of history and made present on every altar of the world."

Archbishop Sheen emphasized that the Eucharist is the continuation of the Cross. To adore it is to adore the Victim who still offers Himself for love of us.

Illustration – A Hidden Adorer

A man who struggled with sin began visiting the Blessed Sacrament daily. Kneeling in silence, he prayed simply: *"Lord, give me strength."* Over time, he discovered that his weakness was being healed at the foot of the tabernacle. Later, he said: *"I found at the altar what I could not find anywhere else — the strength of the Cross alive in the Eucharist."*

His transformation testified that the same power that flowed from Calvary flows still from the altar.

Invitation – Living from the Altar

The Eucharist is not a devotion among others; it is the source and summit of Christian life. To live from the altar is to live from the Cross, drawing strength, healing, and love from Christ's eternal sacrifice.

Ask yourself:

- *Do I approach the Eucharist with the awareness that I am standing at Calvary?*
- *How can I make my Holy Communion an act of deeper surrender to the Crucified Lord?*
- *Am I willing to let the Eucharist shape my life as a continual offering of love?*

Closing Prayer

Lord Jesus, present in the Eucharist, You give me the gift of Calvary made present. Teach me to receive You with reverence, to adore You with love, and to let Your sacrifice become the pattern of my life. May every Communion unite me more deeply to Your Cross and Resurrection.

Amen.

Chapter 15:
The Cross and Eternal Life

Reflection – The Doorway to Glory

For the world, death is the end. For the Christian, the Cross has changed everything. The death of Jesus did not close His story; it opened the way to eternal life.

Through the Cross, sin is conquered and heaven's gates are opened. What once was a symbol of defeat has become the key to paradise. Eternal life is not earned by our strength, but given through the wounds of Christ.

Sheen on Death Transformed

"Before Calvary, death was a prison with no exit. After Calvary, death became a passage — not an end, but a beginning. In the shadow of the Cross, the grave is no longer dark, for it is illumined by the promise of resurrection."

Archbishop Sheen taught that the Cross is the hinge of history: it turns death into life, despair into hope, and time into eternity.

Illustration – The Saint's Confidence

St. Thérèse of Lisieux, near her death, whispered: *"I am not dying, I am entering into life."* Her simple words reveal the truth of the Cross: that eternal life is not an abstract hope but a reality secured by Christ's sacrifice.

Her childlike confidence mirrors the invitation given to the good thief: *"This day you will be with Me in paradise."*

Invitation – Living for Eternity

To live in the light of the Cross is to live with eternity in view. Our choices, our sacrifices, and our sufferings take on new meaning when seen as preparation for the life to come.

Ask yourself:

- *Do I live with my eyes fixed on heaven, or only on this passing world?*
- *How does the Cross shape the way I face suffering and even death?*
- *Am I ready to entrust my life to Christ, confident that His Cross has opened eternal life for me?*

Closing Prayer

Jesus, Lord of life and conqueror of death, through Your Cross You have opened heaven for me. Strengthen my faith in the promise of eternal life. Help me to live each day with heaven in mind, carrying my cross with love, until the day I share in Your glory forever.

Amen.

Chapter 16:
The Cross and Christian Discipleship

Reflection – The Mark of a Disciple

When Jesus called His followers, He did not promise comfort or ease. He said plainly: *"If anyone would come after Me, let him deny himself, take up his cross daily, and follow Me."* (Luke 9:23)

Discipleship is not defined by titles or achievements, but by carrying the Cross in union with Christ. To be His disciple is to walk where He walked — along the way of sacrifice, fidelity, and love that costs something.

Sheen on Following the Crucified

"Our Lord never promised that following Him would mean escaping the Cross. He promised that it would mean carrying one. The Christian life is not immunity from suffering, but communion in suffering — and through it, communion in love."

Archbishop Sheen explained that the mark of an authentic disciple is not success in the world's eyes, but the willingness to follow Christ to Calvary.

Illustration – A Modern Witness

A young man once left a lucrative career to enter the seminary. When asked why, he replied: *"I heard Christ say, 'Take up your cross and follow Me.' I realized that if I gave Him everything, I would gain everything."*

His choice reflected the paradox of discipleship: losing one's life in order to find it.

Invitation – Walking the Narrow Way

Every Christian is called to be a disciple, not in word alone but in daily practice. The Cross is the test of that discipleship — not whether we carry it, but how we carry it: with resentment, or with love.

Ask yourself:

- *What cross is Christ asking me to carry today?*
- *Do I see discipleship as convenience, or as sacrifice?*
- *Am I willing to walk behind Him, even when the road leads to Calvary?*

Closing Prayer

Lord Jesus, You call me to follow You on the way of the Cross. Give me courage to deny myself, strength to carry my burdens, and love to persevere to the end. Make me Your disciple, faithful in trial and joyful in sacrifice, until I share the victory of Your Resurrection.

Amen.

Chapter 17:
The Cross and the Beatitudes

Reflection – The Sermon on the Mount Fulfilled on Calvary

When Jesus first preached the Beatitudes, He blessed the poor, the meek, the merciful, the pure of heart, the persecuted. On Calvary, He lived them all.

The Cross is the ultimate commentary on the Sermon on the Mount. Poverty of spirit is seen in His surrender. Mercy shines in His forgiveness. Purity of heart is revealed in His obedience. Persecution reaches its climax in His death. The Beatitudes are not ideals for the few, but the way of life for every disciple — a way that leads to the Cross.

Sheen on the Paradox of the Beatitudes

"The Beatitudes are not soft virtues for gentle souls; they are the heroic virtues of Christ on the Cross. The world calls them weakness, but Calvary

proves them strength. Blessed are the poor, the meek, the merciful — for they are none other than Christ Himself."

Archbishop Sheen explained that the Beatitudes find their fullest expression at Calvary, where the wisdom of the world is overturned by the wisdom of the Cross.

Illustration – A Hidden Disciple

A missionary once shared the story of a Christian family persecuted for their faith. Despite threats and losses, they remained peaceful, forgiving, and steadfast. *"We would rather lose everything than lose Christ,"* they said.

Their witness reflected the Beatitudes lived in flesh and blood — meekness that was not weakness, mercy that was not naïve, purity of heart that was unshakable.

Invitation – Living the Beatitudes through the Cross

The Beatitudes are not sentimental sayings; they are a road map to Calvary. To live them is to embrace the Cross and to find joy in sacrifice.

Ask yourself:

- *Which Beatitude challenges me the most to live?*
- *How does the Cross give me strength to practice meekness, mercy, or purity of heart?*
- *Am I willing to be "blessed" in the world's eyes as a fool, so that I may be blessed in God's eyes as faithful?*

Closing Prayer

Lord Jesus,
You are the living Beatitude,
poor in spirit, meek and merciful,
pure of heart and persecuted for love.
Teach me to live Your words,
not as distant ideals, but as a daily Cross.
May Your Beatitudes shape my heart,
until I reflect Your love to the world.

Amen.

Chapter 18:
The Cross and the Church

Reflection – Born from the Side of Christ

When the soldier pierced Christ's side, blood and water flowed forth — signs of Baptism and the Eucharist, the sacramental life of the Church. From the wounded Heart of Christ, the Church was born.

The Cross is not only the foundation of individual salvation but also the origin of the Mystical Body. To belong to the Church is to be united to Christ Crucified, sharing in His sufferings and His mission.

Sheen on the Church of Calvary

"The Church is not a society of the perfect but a fellowship of the redeemed, gathered beneath the Cross. Her strength is not her own but flows from the blood that purchased her. To love Christ is to love His Body, the Church."

Archbishop Sheen taught that the Church is inseparable from the Cross. She draws her life, her holiness, and her mission from Calvary itself.

Illustration – The Faith of the Martyrs

In the early Church, Christians gathered in catacombs, risking their lives to celebrate the Eucharist. They carried within them a profound conviction: *"We cannot live without the Lord's Body and Blood."*

Their witness reminds us that the Church is not sustained by human effort but by the sacrifice of Christ, renewed on every altar.

Invitation – Loving the Church at the Foot of the Cross

To belong to the Church is to share both her glory and her wounds. Like the disciples at Calvary, we are called not to abandon her in times of trial but to stand faithfully by her side.

Ask yourself:

- *Do I see the Church as the wounded yet beloved Bride of Christ?*
- *Am I willing to pray, suffer, and labor for her renewal?*
- *How can I live more consciously as a member of the Body born from the Cross?*

Closing Prayer

Lord Jesus, from Your pierced side flowed the life of the Church. Grant me love for Your Body, fidelity in times of trial, and zeal for her mission. May I never leave the foot of the Cross, but remain with Your Bride, sharing in her sufferings until she shares in Your glory.

Amen.

Chapter 19:
The Cross and the Priesthood

Reflection – The Altar of Sacrifice

At the Last Supper, Jesus instituted both the Eucharist and the priesthood. On Calvary, He consummated that gift by offering Himself as the eternal High Priest and Victim. Every priest shares in this mystery: he is ordained not for privilege, but for sacrifice.

The Cross reveals that the priesthood is not a career but a crucifixion. To stand at the altar is to stand at Calvary, offering not only bread and wine, but one's very life in union with Christ.

Sheen on the Priest and the Cross

"The priest is called not merely to offer the Cross, but to be on it. Every Mass he celebrates is a personal invitation to die with Christ, that others may live. The world will understand him only when it sees in him the shadow of Calvary."

Archbishop Sheen insisted that the priesthood cannot be understood apart from sacrifice. The priest is configured to Christ the Victim, and his fruitfulness flows from his willingness to be nailed with Him.

Illustration – A Hidden Shepherd

During persecution in Eastern Europe, priests secretly celebrated the Mass in barns and basements. Many were arrested, some martyred. One survivor later wrote: *"We were not heroes. We were priests. This is what priests do – we offer, even if it costs our lives."*

Their fidelity revealed the essence of the priesthood: to make Christ present through the Cross, no matter the cost.

Invitation – Praying for Priests

Every Christian is called to pray for priests, that they may remain faithful to their vocation of sacrifice. And in a broader sense, every baptized soul shares in Christ's priesthood, called to offer daily life as a spiritual sacrifice to God.

Ask yourself:

- *Do I pray regularly for priests, especially those burdened or tempted?*
- *How can I live my baptismal priesthood by offering my daily crosses in union with Christ?*
- *Am I willing to see the priesthood not only as ministry, but as Calvary made present?*

Closing Prayer

Lord Jesus, Eternal High Priest, sanctify Your priests in the fire of Your love. Grant them fidelity to the Cross, courage in sacrifice, and joy in service. Teach me also, through my baptism, to offer my life as a holy sacrifice, united to Yours at every Mass.

Amen.

Chapter 20:
The Cross and Reparation

Reflection – Love That Repairs

Sin is not only the breaking of a law but the wounding of love. Every sin offends the Heart of God. At Calvary, Jesus offered Himself not only to forgive sin but to repair the damage it caused — to restore what was broken, to heal what was wounded, to make love whole again.

Reparation is our response to that love. To make reparation is to console the Heart of Christ by uniting our prayers, sacrifices, and fidelity to His Cross.

Sheen on the Need for Reparation

"Sin is not something impersonal; it nailed Him to the Cross. Reparation is not something abstract; it is the return of love for love. To do reparation is to stand with Christ at Calvary and say: 'I will not leave You alone.'"

Archbishop Sheen explained that reparation is love's answer to the world's indifference. If sin forgets God, reparation remembers Him.

Illustration – The Hidden Consoler

St. Thérèse of Lisieux once said: *"I choose all."* She meant that she would accept every small suffering as a way of consoling Jesus. Whether misunderstood by her sisters or enduring physical pain, she transformed each trial into an act of love.

Her Little Way shows us that reparation is not reserved for great penances; it is lived in hidden fidelity, day by day, for love of Christ.

Invitation – Sharing in Christ's Work

To make reparation is to let our lives become a living "yes" to God's love, repairing the "no" of sin. It may mean offering our sufferings, praying before the Eucharist, or performing small acts of love done with great faith.

Ask yourself:

- *What act of love can I offer today to console the Heart of Christ?*
- *Do I see my daily sacrifices as useless, or as opportunities to repair what sin has wounded?*
- *How can I be a consoler of Jesus in a world that often forgets Him?*

Closing Prayer

O Jesus, You bore the weight of sin upon the Cross. I offer You my prayers, my sacrifices, my love, to console Your Heart and to repair what sin has broken. Teach me to live each day in reparation, that my life may return love for love, until the world is renewed in Your mercy.

Amen.

Chapter 21:
The Cross and Hope

Reflection – Light in the Midst of Darkness

From the outside, Calvary looked like defeat. The disciples scattered, the enemies mocked, and the sky itself grew dark. Yet from that darkest hour came the dawn of Easter. The Cross is the paradox of Christian hope: when all seems lost, God is nearest.

Hope does not deny suffering; it transforms it. To hope in the Cross is to believe that God can draw life from death, light from darkness, victory from apparent failure.

Sheen on the Certainty of Hope

"Despair sees only the nails; hope sees the hands that are nailed. Despair sees only the thorns; hope sees the brow that wears them as a crown. The Cross is the anchor of hope, because it reveals that God's love is stronger than our sins and greater than our deaths."

Archbishop Sheen emphasized that hope is not optimism or wishful thinking. It is the confidence that Christ's victory is already won, even when hidden beneath the Cross.

Illustration – A Prisoner's Song

A Christian imprisoned for his faith endured years of darkness with no sign of release. Yet each night, he softly sang hymns of hope. Asked later how he endured, he replied: *"They could chain my body, but not my hope in Christ."*

Like the thief promised paradise, he discovered that even behind bars, the Cross radiates hope that cannot be silenced.

Invitation – Choosing Hope Daily

The Cross confronts us with two choices: despair or hope. To choose hope is to cling to the promises of God when feelings fade, when prayers seem unanswered, when life feels heavy. It is to whisper, "I trust You, Lord," even in the dark.

Ask yourself:

- *Where am I tempted to despair today?*
- *Do I see my Cross as the end of hope, or as the very reason for it?*
- *How can I bear witness to Christian hope in a world that often gives in to despair?*

Closing Prayer

Lord of Calvary and Easter, anchor my heart in hope. When trials weigh me down, lift my eyes to Your Cross. When despair whispers its lies, remind me of Your victory. May I live as a witness that the Cross is never the end, but always the doorway to glory.

Amen.

Chapter 22:
The Cross and Love

Reflection – Love Revealed in Full

Love is often spoken of lightly, but on Calvary it is revealed in its truest form. The Cross is love stretched to its limit — a love willing to suffer, to forgive, to give all, holding nothing back.

At the Cross, Jesus shows that love is not sentiment but sacrifice. The measure of love is not how much it feels, but how much it gives.

Sheen on the Measure of Love

"The proof of love is sacrifice. He who loves much, suffers much. The Cross is not only the sign of our redemption; it is the sign of what love costs. And unless love costs something, it is not love."

Archbishop Sheen insisted that the Cross is both revelation and invitation: revelation of how much God loves us, and invitation to love in the same way.

Illustration – A Mother's Gift

A mother who cared for her sick child around the clock was once asked how she found the strength. She replied simply: *"When you love, nothing is too much."*

Her words echoed the heart of Calvary, where Christ gave everything for love, never counting the cost.

Invitation – Learning to Love at the Cross

To live beneath the Cross is to let it redefine love in our lives — in marriages, families, friendships, and communities. Love will always cost something: time, comfort, pride. But in giving, we discover joy.

Ask yourself:

- *Do I measure love by what I receive, or by what I give?*
- *Where is Christ inviting me to love sacrificially today?*
- *Am I willing to let the Cross be the standard of my love?*

Closing Prayer

Crucified Love, teach me to love as You love. Empty me of selfishness, fill me with generosity, and give me the courage to sacrifice with joy. May my love be measured not by words, but by the Cross I bear with You.

Amen.

Chapter 23:
The Cross and the Christian Life

Reflection – The Pattern of Every Disciple

The Cross is not only Christ's mission; it is the pattern of the entire Christian life. To follow Him is to take up our own cross daily. Not as punishment, but as participation in His love.

The Christian life is not about avoiding suffering at all costs, but about allowing even our trials to become offerings of love. Calvary becomes the lens through which we see every moment of life — work, family, sacrifice, and prayer.

Sheen on the Christian Vocation

"Christianity without a Cross is a lie. Our Lord did not invite us to a path of comfort but to a road of sacrifice. The Christian who would avoid the Cross will avoid Christ Himself, for He is never found apart from it."

Archbishop Sheen taught that holiness is not achieved by running from suffering, but by embracing it in union with Christ. The Cross is both the cost and the glory of discipleship.

Illustration – A Quiet Witness

A woman caring for her elderly parents once admitted: *"Some days I feel overwhelmed. But when I look at the crucifix, I remember that my small crosses can become prayers, too."*

Her hidden fidelity became a living example of the Christian life: ordinary sacrifice transformed into extraordinary grace by the Cross.

Invitation – Living the Cross Daily

Every Christian is invited to see life itself as a participation in Calvary. The question is not whether we will suffer, but whether we will suffer with Christ or without Him.

Ask yourself:

- *Do I see my daily duties and sacrifices as part of the Cross of Christ?*
- *How can I turn ordinary struggles into offerings of love?*
- *Am I willing to live my whole life in the light of Calvary?*

Closing Prayer

Lord Jesus, make my life a reflection of Your Cross. Let my words, my work, my joys, and my sorrows all be united to You. Teach me to carry my cross daily with love, so that my whole life may proclaim: "I live, now not I, but Christ lives in me."

Amen.

Chapter 24:
The Cross and the Saints

Reflection – Holiness Shaped by the Cross

Every saint bears the imprint of Calvary. Their sanctity did not come from escaping suffering, but from embracing it with love. From martyrs in the arena to cloistered nuns in hidden silence, the saints teach us that the Cross is the path to glory.

The Cross purifies, strengthens, and transforms. It is the school where holiness is learned and the fire where love is proved.

Sheen on the Saints of Calvary

"The saints are those who loved the Cross, not because suffering is good in itself, but because it is the seal of Christ's love. Every saint has stood at Calvary, some with blood, others with tears, all with love."

Archbishop Sheen reminded us that sanctity is impossible without the Cross. To admire Christ without sharing His suffering is to stop short of true discipleship.

Illustration – St. Francis and the Crucified

St. Francis of Assisi prayed: *"My God and my all."* His love for the Crucified became so deep that he bore the stigmata — the wounds of Christ in his own body. His life reminds us that the Cross is not distant history but a present reality that can shape a soul completely.

The saints may differ in culture, age, and vocation, but all are united by this: they loved the Cross.

Invitation – Walking the Same Path

Holiness is not reserved for the few but offered to all. The saints prove that the Cross can be carried in every circumstance: in family life, in work, in suffering, in prayer. To imitate them is to join the great procession of souls following Christ to Calvary.

Ask yourself:

- *Do I look to the saints as models of embracing the Cross with love?*
- *Which saint inspires me most to carry my own cross faithfully?*
- *Am I willing to let my trials become the forge of sanctity in my life?*

Closing Prayer

Lord of the saints, You crowned their lives with the glory of the Cross. Teach me to follow their example, to love You in sacrifice, and to remain faithful in trial. May I one day join their company, sharing forever in the victory of Your love.

Amen.

Chapter 25:
The Cross and Eternal Glory

Reflection – From Suffering to Splendor

The Cross, once a symbol of shame, has become the throne of glory. By embracing suffering in love, Christ turned death into life and defeat into victory. The wood of the Cross became the ladder to heaven.

For the Christian, this means that every cross carried faithfully is crowned with glory. Our sufferings are not the final word — they are transformed into eternal joy when united with the sacrifice of Christ.

Sheen on Glory Through the Cross

"There is no Easter Sunday without Good Friday. The world seeks glory without sacrifice, but Christ shows that glory comes only through the Cross. He who climbs Calvary with Christ will one day share His crown."

Archbishop Sheen often reminded us that the saints shine brightest because they first embraced the shadows of the Cross. Their eternal reward was born from temporal sacrifice.

Illustration – A Martyr's Crown

St. Ignatius of Antioch, on his way to martyrdom, wrote: *"Let me be ground like wheat in the teeth of wild beasts, that I may become the pure bread of Christ."* His hope was not in escaping suffering, but in the eternal glory that awaited him through the Cross.

His courage shows that the Cross does not diminish life; it enlarges it into eternity.

Invitation – Lifting Our Eyes to Heaven

In moments of trial, the Cross invites us to lift our gaze beyond present pain to the glory to come. Fidelity now prepares us for joy without end.

Ask yourself:

- *Do I see my crosses only as burdens, or also as pathways to eternal glory?*
- *How does the promise of heaven give me strength to endure trials today?*
- *Am I willing to trust that every sacrifice united with Christ will be rewarded in eternity?*

Closing Prayer

Lord of Glory, through the Cross You have opened heaven. Strengthen me to endure my trials with hope, knowing that eternal joy awaits. May every burden I bear in faith be crowned one day with the splendor of Your presence. Let my life proclaim: "Through the Cross to glory."

Amen.

Chapter 26:
The Cross and Our Daily Mission

Reflection – Sent from Calvary

The Cross does not only call us to faith — it sends us on mission. From the pierced Heart of Christ flowed blood and water, signs of the sacraments through which the Church was born and sent. Every Christian mission begins at Calvary.

To live our mission is to carry the Cross into the world: into homes, workplaces, friendships, and even hostile places. Our witness is not persuasive words alone but lives shaped by sacrificial love.

Sheen on Apostolic Mission

"The greatest tragedy in the world is not suffering, but wasted suffering. If we unite our daily trials to the Cross, then they become apostolic — they redeem, they teach, they convert. The Cross carried in love becomes the seed of mission."

Archbishop Sheen taught that our mission is not apart from the Cross, but born from it. Evangelization is credible when the world sees love that suffers and yet still forgives.

Illustration – A Lay Apostle

A factory worker quietly carried a rosary in his pocket. During breaks, he prayed for his co-workers, offering his long hours as a sacrifice for their souls. Over time, several colleagues returned to the sacraments through his hidden witness.

His mission was not loud or public, but rooted in the Cross lived daily in faithfulness.

Invitation – Carrying the Cross into the World

Each of us has a mission field — our family, workplace, parish, neighborhood. To bring the Cross there is to live sacrificially, to forgive generously, to love when it costs something.

Ask yourself:

- *Where is Christ sending me to be a witness of His Cross?*
- *Do I see my daily struggles as obstacles, or as opportunities for mission?*
- *How can my fidelity become an instrument of grace for others?*

Closing Prayer

Lord Jesus, You sent Your disciples from Calvary to the ends of the earth. Send me into my daily mission with the power of Your Cross. Make my sacrifices fruitful, my prayers apostolic, and my love a witness to Your mercy. May I carry Your Cross into the world, so that others may find life in You.

Amen.

Chapter 27:
The Cross and Victory

Reflection – Triumph in Apparent Defeat

On Calvary, Jesus looked like a defeated man: mocked by enemies, abandoned by friends, nailed to a cross. Yet it was precisely there, in the world's darkest hour, that victory was won. Sin was conquered, death was broken, and Satan's power was crushed.

The Cross teaches us that Christian victory does not come through force or domination but through love that suffers and forgives. What looks like loss in the eyes of the world is triumph in the eyes of God.

Sheen on the Paradox of Victory

"The world thought it had heard the last of Christ on Calvary. But it was only the beginning. The very act by which His enemies triumphed was the act by which He triumphed over them. The Cross is not failure — it is victory."

Archbishop Sheen reminded us that the victory of the Cross is quiet yet cosmic, hidden yet eternal. It is the triumph of love over hate, mercy over sin, life over death.

Illustration – A Martyr's Witness

During the early persecutions, Christians often entered the arena singing hymns. To the crowds, their deaths looked like defeat. Yet their joyful surrender inspired conversions across the empire. Their blood became, in Tertullian's famous words, "the seed of the Church."

Their apparent loss was, in truth, the victory of the Cross shining through them.

Invitation – Sharing in Christ's Triumph

We, too, face battles — with sin, discouragement, and temptation. The Cross assures us that victory is already won, though we may not see it yet. Our task is to remain faithful, confident that Christ's triumph will be revealed in us.

Ask yourself:

- *Do I view my struggles as hopeless defeats, or as arenas where Christ's victory can shine?*
- *Am I willing to trust that the Cross has already conquered my greatest fears?*
- *How can I live each day as a witness to Christ's triumph?*

Closing Prayer

Victorious Lord, Your Cross is my hope and my triumph. Help me to trust that no defeat is final when it is united to You. Grant me courage in trial, confidence in Your mercy, and joy in the victory of love. May my life proclaim: "The Cross is victory."

Amen.

Chapter 28:
The Cross and Peace

Reflection – Peace Born from Sacrifice

The world often defines peace as the absence of conflict, comfort, or control. But the Cross reveals a deeper peace — the peace of reconciliation. By His sacrifice, Christ broke down the wall between God and humanity, making peace through the blood of His Cross (Colossians 1:20).

True peace does not ignore suffering; it is born from it. At Calvary, mercy and justice met, and in their embrace, peace was born for the world.

Sheen on Christ the Peace-Maker

"Peace is not merely a truce between enemies; it is the restoration of order through love. Christ brought peace not by avoiding the Cross, but by embracing it. His wounds healed our rebellion, and His death reconciled earth with heaven."

Archbishop Sheen reminded us that peace cannot come from politics, possessions, or power. It flows only from the pierced Heart of Christ.

Illustration – Forgiveness Restores Peace

A man once forgave the drunk driver who had caused the death of his daughter. When asked how, he answered: *"I looked at the crucifix and remembered how much I have been forgiven."*

His act of mercy did not erase his loss, but it gave him peace — the kind of peace that only the Cross can give.

Invitation – Becoming Instruments of Peace

To live beneath the Cross is to become a peacemaker. This does not mean avoiding conflict at any cost, but healing divisions with love and forgiveness. The Cross calls us to bring reconciliation where there is hatred, and hope where there is despair.

Ask yourself:

- *Do I seek peace only in comfort, or in the deeper reconciliation Christ offers?*
- *Where is God asking me to be an instrument of peace – in my family, my parish, my community?*
- *Am I willing to forgive as I have been forgiven?*

Closing Prayer

Lord Jesus, Prince of Peace, by the blood of Your Cross, You reconciled the world to the Father. Heal the divisions in my heart, my family, and my community. Make me an instrument of Your peace, bearing Your mercy where there is hurt, and Your hope where there is despair. Let my life echo Your gift of peace poured out from Calvary.

Amen.

Chapter 29:
The Cross and Joy

Reflection – Joy Hidden in Sorrow

At first glance, the Cross seems the opposite of joy. It is a place of pain, loss, and humiliation. Yet hidden within its sorrow is a deeper joy — the joy of love fulfilled, of obedience carried to the end, of redemption accomplished.

Christian joy is not the denial of suffering but the discovery of meaning within it. The Cross shows us that joy and sorrow are not enemies; when united to Christ, sorrow becomes the seed of joy.

Sheen on Joy Through the Cross

"Joy is not the avoidance of the Cross, but the embrace of it. The world promises happiness in pleasures; Christ promises joy in sacrifice. And His promise endures, for the Cross leads not to despair but to resurrection."

Archbishop Sheen explained that Christian joy is the serene confidence that love is stronger than death. It is the peace of knowing that Calvary ends in Easter.

Illustration – Joy in the Midst of Trial

St. Teresa of Calcutta often smiled even in the midst of exhaustion and trial. When asked how, she replied: *"Joy is prayer; joy is strength; joy is love. Joy is love with a smile."*

Her joy was not superficial. It flowed from the Cross — from seeing Christ in the poor, serving Him in sacrifice, and trusting Him in suffering.

Invitation – Choosing Joy in the Cross

Joy is a choice, not a feeling. Each day, we can choose to see the Cross not as an obstacle but as a gift — the place where God's love meets our lives.

Ask yourself:

- *Do I equate joy with comfort, or do I seek it in the love of Christ crucified?*
- *Where can I bring joy into the lives of others through sacrifice and love?*
- *Am I willing to let the Cross transform my sorrows into seeds of joy?*

Closing Prayer

Lord Jesus, You endured the Cross for the joy set before You. Teach me to find joy not in avoiding sacrifice, but in embracing it with love. Let my heart be filled with Easter joy even in Good Friday trials, so that my life may shine with the gladness of the Gospel.

Amen.

Chapter 30:
The Cross and the Christian Home

Reflection – The Cross at the Heart of Family Life

The home is often called the "domestic church." It is the place where love is learned, sacrifices are made, and faith is handed on. Yet no home is without its crosses — misunderstandings, hardships, illnesses, or daily struggles.

When the Cross is welcomed into the home, it becomes not a source of division but of unity. Shared sacrifice binds hearts together and opens the door for Christ to dwell in the midst of the family.

Sheen on Family and the Cross

"The Christian home is built not merely on human love but on divine love. And divine love is always marked by the Cross. A family that refuses sacrifice will not endure; a family that embraces it will find strength beyond its own."

Archbishop Sheen taught that the Cross sanctifies family life, transforming ordinary duties into acts of grace and daily struggles into opportunities for holiness.

Illustration – A Family's Hidden Fidelity

A father working two jobs to provide for his children, a mother caring for the sick with patience, siblings learning to forgive quarrels — these may seem small in the world's eyes, but in God's eyes they are acts of Calvary lived at home.

Such hidden sacrifices, offered with love, make the home an altar where Christ's Cross is present and fruitful.

Invitation – Making the Home a Sanctuary of Love

Every home can reflect Calvary by turning sacrifice into love and challenges into opportunities for grace. A crucifix on the wall is not only a decoration but a reminder that Christ is the unseen Guest in every room.

Ask yourself:

- *Do I welcome Christ and His Cross into my home, or do I resist it?*
- *How can I transform daily family sacrifices into offerings of love?*
- *Am I helping my home to be a place where Christ is known, loved, and served?*

Closing Prayer

Lord Jesus, make my home a reflection of Your Cross. Bless my family with patience in trial, forgiveness in conflict, and love in sacrifice. May our home be a sanctuary where Your presence is felt and Your Cross is embraced with faith.

Amen.

Chapter 31:
The Cross and the World

Reflection – The Cross as the Axis of History

The Cross is not only the center of Christian life; it is the hinge of history. On Calvary, the world was judged and redeemed. All nations, cultures, and generations must confront its challenge: will we see the Cross as folly, or as the wisdom and power of God (1 Corinthians 1:18)?

The Cross stands above every age, uniting what is good, exposing what is false, and offering hope to a world in need of redemption.

Sheen on the Cross in History

"The Cross is the axis around which the universe turns. Empires rise and fall, philosophies come and go, but the Cross endures. It is the one sign that the world cannot escape, for in it lies both its judgment and its salvation."

Archbishop Sheen often said that the Cross is not only personal but cosmic. It redeems not just individuals but the entire world.

Illustration – The Power of the Cross Across Nations

Missionaries in distant lands have found that even where cultures differ, the Cross speaks a universal language. One missionary told of a village that rejected all foreign customs but welcomed the crucifix, saying: *"This God knows our suffering."*

The Cross is the meeting point where every people and culture can recognize their story fulfilled in Christ.

Invitation – Bearing the Cross for the World

Each Christian is called to see beyond personal salvation to the salvation of the world. By uniting our sacrifices to Christ, we join in His work of redeeming all peoples and nations.

Ask yourself:

- *Do I see the Cross only as my personal consolation, or as God's gift for the whole world?*
- *How can I witness to Christ's love in a culture that often rejects Him?*
- *Am I willing to carry my share of the world's suffering in prayer and sacrifice?*

Closing Prayer

Lord of the nations, Your Cross is the hope of the world. Bring peace where there is war, truth where there is error, and love where there is hatred. Use my life, my prayers, and my sacrifices to extend the shadow of Your Cross across the whole earth, until every knee bows before You.

Amen.

Chapter 32:
The Cross and the Christian Apostolate

Reflection – Mission Flows from the Cross

Every apostolate — whether preaching, teaching, serving, or praying — finds its source at Calvary. The apostle is not primarily a strategist or organizer, but a witness to the love poured out on the Cross.

The fruitfulness of any mission does not depend on human talent alone but on union with Christ crucified. Without the Cross, the apostolate becomes activism; with the Cross, it becomes redemptive.

Sheen on Apostolic Zeal

"The world is not saved by brilliant men, but by crucified ones. Our Lord chose not the learned of the world, but those willing to leave all and take up their cross. The apostle is great not because of what he does, but because of how much of Christ's Cross he carries."

Archbishop Sheen reminded us that the power of Christian witness comes from sacrifice. Apostolic zeal is born not of ambition, but of love that is willing to suffer.

Illustration – A Missionary's Secret

A missionary once confessed that the key to his ministry's fruitfulness was not his words, but his hidden hours before the Blessed Sacrament. He said: *"I preached with my lips, but I wept with Christ for souls before the altar. That was my real mission."*

His testimony reveals that the apostolate without prayer and sacrifice is empty, but with the Cross, it becomes life-giving.

Invitation – Making My Life Apostolic

Every Christian is an apostle in some way — in the family, the parish, the workplace, the wider world. Our witness is powerful when it springs from the Cross.

Ask yourself:

- *Do I see my mission as my own work, or as Christ's work through me?*
- *How can I root my apostolic efforts more deeply in prayer and sacrifice?*
- *Am I willing to let my life become a living sermon of the Cross?*

Closing Prayer

Lord of the harvest, make me an apostle of Your Cross. Give me zeal rooted in sacrifice, strength born of prayer, and courage born of love. May all my efforts bear fruit, not for my glory but for Yours, so that the world may know the power of the Cross.

Amen.

Chapter 33:
The Cross and the Mystical Body

Reflection – One Body, Sharing One Cross

On Calvary, Christ did not suffer for Himself but for His Body — the Church. By Baptism, we are grafted into Him, made members of His Mystical Body. This means the Cross is no longer His alone; it is ours.

When one member suffers, all suffer; when one is honored, all rejoice (1 Corinthians 12:26). The Cross binds us together in a communion of love, sacrifice, and mission.

Sheen on the Unity of the Body

"The Cross is not only Christ's; it belongs to His Body, the Church. Every Christian must fill up what is lacking in the sufferings of Christ — not because His work was incomplete, but because His love is so great that He allows us to share in it."

Archbishop Sheen emphasized that Christ invites His members to join their sufferings with His, so that His redemptive love may reach every soul.

Illustration – A Chain of Grace

A cloistered nun, unseen by the world, offered her daily sufferings for missionaries in the field. Those missionaries, in turn, brought the Gospel to villages that had never heard of Christ. Souls were saved because one hidden member of the Body carried her cross in love.

Her example shows how the Cross unites us in a chain of grace that stretches across the world.

Invitation – Sharing in the Sufferings of Christ

To belong to the Mystical Body is to bear one another's burdens, offering our crosses not only for ourselves but for the salvation of others.

Ask yourself:

- *Do I see my sufferings as isolated, or as joined to the Body of Christ?*
- *Whom can I consciously carry in prayer through the weight of my cross?*
- *Am I willing to unite my sacrifices to Christ for the sake of His Church?*

Closing Prayer

Lord Jesus, Head of the Body, teach me to suffer and to love with You. Unite my small crosses to Your great sacrifice, so that grace may flow to others. Make me a faithful member of Your Mystical Body, sharing in its sorrows and its joys, until we are one with You in glory.

Amen.

Chapter 34:
The Cross and the Sacraments

Reflection – Channels from Calvary

When Jesus died on the Cross, blood and water flowed from His pierced side — signs of the sacraments that would spring forth from His sacrifice. Baptism cleanses us in that water, the Eucharist nourishes us with that blood, and the other sacraments draw their power from the same fountain of grace.

The sacraments are not human rituals but divine streams flowing directly from Calvary, carrying the fruits of redemption into every generation.

Sheen on the Sacramental Life

"The Cross is the fountainhead of the sacraments. They are the continuation of Calvary through time. Each sacrament applies the fruits of the Passion to our souls, making us contemporaries of the saving act of Christ."

Archbishop Sheen emphasized that the sacraments unite us to the Cross in real, tangible ways. In every Baptism, Confirmation, Confession, Eucharist, Matrimony, Ordination, and Anointing, Calvary is present.

Illustration – The Power of Confession

A man burdened by years of sin entered the confessional with trembling. When the priest pronounced absolution, he later said: *"I felt as if the weight of the Cross itself had lifted me up."*

His experience reflected the truth that in every sacrament, the grace of the Cross touches individual lives with healing and power.

Invitation – Living from the Sacraments

The sacraments are not optional extras but the ordinary means by which we live the mystery of the Cross. To receive them is to drink from the side of Christ and to be renewed in His sacrifice.

Ask yourself:

- *Do I approach the sacraments as routine, or as encounters with the Cross?*
- *How can I deepen my preparation and thanksgiving for each sacrament I receive?*
- *Am I letting the grace of Calvary, poured out in the sacraments, transform my daily life?*

Closing Prayer

Lord Jesus, from Your pierced side flowed the sacraments of the Church. Grant me reverence when I approach them, gratitude when I receive them, and fidelity in living their grace. Through them, may my life be ever united to Your Cross and open to Your Resurrection.

Amen.

Chapter 35:
The Cross and Mary

Reflection – The Mother at Calvary

No one stood closer to the mystery of the Cross than Mary. She shared not in the physical nails or scourging, but in the agony of a pierced heart. At Calvary, she became not only the Mother of Jesus but the Mother of all the redeemed.

Her presence at the Cross reminds us that discipleship is not only about doing, but about standing — remaining faithful, even when the sword pierces the soul.

Sheen on Mary at the Cross

"Mary was not merely a spectator at Calvary. She was a co-sufferer. As Jesus gave His Body, she gave her Son. As He offered His life, she offered her maternal heart. In her we see the perfect disciple who never turned away from the Cross."

Archbishop Sheen taught that Mary's greatest act of faith was not at Nazareth, but at Calvary — trusting God even when His plan seemed most hidden.

Illustration – A Mother's Silent Strength

A mother caring for her son battling addiction once said: *"I cannot take his cross away, but I can stand beside him."*

Her words echo Mary at Calvary, who could not remove the nails but could remain faithful. Her silent strength became her son's greatest consolation.

Invitation – Taking Mary into Our Lives

From the Cross, Jesus entrusted Mary to John, and John to Mary. Each of us is invited to do the same — to take her into our homes, our hearts, our struggles. She teaches us how to remain at the Cross without despair and how to love even in suffering.

Ask yourself:

- *Have I welcomed Mary as my Mother, especially in times of trial?*
- *Do I turn to her for consolation and strength at the foot of my own crosses?*
- *Am I willing to let her teach me how to stand faithfully with Christ?*

Closing Prayer

Mary, Mother of Sorrows, teach me to stand with you at the Cross. Help me to offer my sufferings with love, to trust when I do not understand, and to remain faithful when trials come. Be my Mother, my comfort, and my guide, until I share forever in the victory of your Son.

Amen.

Chapter 36:
The Cross and the Mass

Reflection – Calvary Made Present

The Mass is not a mere remembrance of Calvary, but its living presence. At every altar, the sacrifice of the Cross is renewed in an unbloody manner. We are not transported back in time; rather, the mystery of Calvary is brought into our time and place.

To attend Mass, then, is to stand once more at the foot of the Cross with Mary and John. It is to see love poured out and to join our lives to that offering.

Sheen on the Mass as Sacrifice

"The Mass is Calvary without distance of space or time. The same Christ is present, the same sacrifice is offered, the same love is poured out. The difference is only this: on Calvary He was alone; at the Mass we are invited to offer ourselves with Him."

Archbishop Sheen insisted that the Mass is not primarily about receiving, but about offering — uniting our lives, joys, and sorrows with Christ's perfect oblation.

Illustration – A Hidden Offering

A parishioner once whispered before Mass: *"I place my whole week on the altar."* Her struggles at work, her worries for her children, her hidden sacrifices — all became part of the bread and wine, lifted up with Christ's Cross to the Father.

Her witness reveals that when we unite our lives to the Mass, nothing is wasted.

Invitation – Living the Mass Beyond the Altar

The Mass does not end at the dismissal; it begins anew in our daily lives. What we have offered at the altar, we must live in the world. To live Eucharistically is to carry the Cross into every corner of life.

Ask yourself:

- *Do I approach Mass as a true encounter with Calvary, or only as a ritual?*
- *What can I consciously place on the altar at my next Mass?*
- *Am I living what I celebrate — making my life an offering united to Christ's?*

Closing Prayer

Lord Jesus, at every Mass You renew the gift of Calvary. Teach me to come with reverence, to offer myself with You, and to live each day as a Eucharistic sacrifice. May I never forget that the altar is the Cross, and that in Your sacrifice I find my life.

Amen.

Chapter 37:
The Cross and Christian Virtue

Reflection – Virtue Tested in Fire

Virtue is not formed in comfort but in trial. Patience, humility, courage, and charity grow when tested by the weight of the Cross. Calvary is the forge where Christian virtue is purified and perfected.

The Cross shows us that virtue is not simply about self-improvement but about self-giving. It is love in action, even when it costs something.

Sheen on Virtue from the Cross

"The virtues are not abstract qualities but Christ Himself living in us. Patience is His patience in our trials, humility is His humility in our struggles, charity is His charity in our sacrifices. Virtue flows not from willpower alone but from union with the Cross."

Archbishop Sheen taught that the Cross transforms natural strengths into supernatural virtues by rooting them in love.

Illustration – Patience in Trial

A man caring for his bedridden wife was once asked how he bore the burden. He answered: *"Every day I look at the crucifix and remember: love is patient. If He endured for me, I can endure for her."*

His patience was not weakness but strength born at Calvary — a living virtue shaped by the Cross.

Invitation – Practicing Virtue Daily

Every day brings opportunities to grow in virtue: to choose humility over pride, forgiveness over resentment, patience over anger, generosity over selfishness. The Cross makes these choices possible by giving us the strength of Christ Himself.

Ask yourself:

- *Which virtue is God asking me to cultivate right now?*
- *Do I rely only on my own strength, or do I draw from the grace of the Cross?*
- *How can I practice small acts of virtue each day, rooted in love?*

Closing Prayer

Lord Jesus, You are the perfection of every virtue. Form in me patience, humility, courage, and charity through the trials I face. May the Cross be my teacher, and may my life reflect Your virtues, until I shine with Your likeness.

Amen.

Chapter 38:
The Cross and the Christian Nation

Reflection – A People Under the Cross

Nations, like individuals, rise or fall by how they relate to the Cross. A Christian nation is not one without suffering, but one that interprets its trials in the light of Calvary. When the Cross is honored, justice and mercy flourish; when it is rejected, selfishness and division reign.

The health of a society is measured not by wealth or power but by whether it is willing to sacrifice for the common good, just as Christ sacrificed for all.

Sheen on the Cross and Society

"The Cross is not only the salvation of souls but the salvation of civilization. A nation that forgets the Cross will die of its own selfishness; a nation that remembers it will endure through sacrifice and love."

Archbishop Sheen warned that when societies abandon the Cross, they also abandon truth and charity. But when they embrace it, they are renewed in justice, compassion, and peace.

Illustration – Renewal in Hardship

After a devastating war, a small village rebuilt its church, beginning with the crucifix that had survived the destruction. Families carried stones, children gathered wood, elders prayed aloud. That crucifix reminded them that only through the Cross could their community be restored.

Their faith bore witness that the Cross is not only personal but national, capable of renewing whole peoples.

Invitation – Bearing the Cross for the Common Good

As Christians, we are called to bring the Cross into our civic life — through honesty, sacrifice, service, and the defense of truth. A nation grows strong when its citizens live the virtues of Calvary.

Ask yourself:

- *Do I see my role in society as shaped by the Cross?*
- *How can I bring sacrificial love into my community and nation?*
- *Am I willing to suffer for truth and justice, even when unpopular?*

Closing Prayer

Lord of nations, place my country beneath the shadow of Your Cross. Heal our divisions, renew our leaders in wisdom, and strengthen our people in virtue. May we be a nation willing to sacrifice for love, and may the Cross be our guide and our glory.

Amen.

Chapter 39:
The Cross and Perseverance

Reflection – Enduring to the End

The Christian life is not a sprint but a pilgrimage. Along the way, many grow weary, some turn back, and others stumble. The Cross teaches us that victory is not found in starting well, but in finishing faithfully.

Jesus carried His Cross to the very end. Perseverance is the virtue of remaining steady beneath the weight of trial until love has completed its work.

Sheen on Perseverance at Calvary

"Our Lord did not come down from the Cross when taunted. He endured until the sacrifice was complete. Perseverance is the mark of true love – not to love only when it is easy, but to love until the very end."

Archbishop Sheen reminded us that perseverance is the proof of authentic faith. To endure faithfully in trials is to mirror Christ's own fidelity.

Illustration – A Steadfast Soul

A woman who prayed daily for her wayward son did not give up, even after decades without change. Near the end of her life, he returned to the sacraments. She said simply: *"I just kept carrying the cross for him."*

Her perseverance reflected the patient endurance of Calvary, where love refuses to give up.

Invitation – Remaining Faithful in Trial

The Cross invites us to steadfastness. Perseverance is not stubbornness but fidelity — the refusal to abandon Christ when the road grows hard.

Ask yourself:

- *Where am I tempted to give up in faith, prayer, or duty?*
- *Do I carry my cross only when light, or also when heavy?*
- *Am I willing to endure to the end, trusting in Christ's victory?*

Closing Prayer

Lord Jesus, You persevered to the end upon the Cross. Strengthen me when I grow weary, sustain me when I am tempted to quit, and keep me faithful in love. May I finish the race, carry the Cross to the end, and share in the crown of life You promise.

Amen.

Chapter 40:
The Cross and Final Perseverance

Reflection – The Grace of a Faithful End

Life is filled with many beginnings, but what matters most is how we end. Final perseverance is the grace to remain faithful to Christ until our last breath. At Calvary, Jesus showed us how to die — not in despair, but in surrender, entrusting His spirit into the Father's hands.

The Cross teaches us that the Christian's last act is not defeat but offering — returning our life to the One who gave it.

Sheen on Persevering to the End

"In the end, men are judged not by the beginnings of their lives but by their closings. Judas began well, Peter began poorly; but Peter ended well, and Judas ended badly. Final perseverance is the crowning grace, and it is won at the foot of the Cross."

Archbishop Sheen reminded us that no matter how weak our past has been, the grace of final perseverance is always possible — if we remain close to the Crucified.

Illustration – A Holy Death

A priest once kept vigil at the bedside of a dying woman. Though she had suffered much, her final words were: *"Into Your hands, O Lord."* With the crucifix in her hand, she surrendered her spirit in peace.

Her holy death bore witness that the Cross prepares us not only for life but for eternity.

Invitation – Preparing for the Last Hour

Every day is preparation for the final surrender. To live well is to die well. If we carry our crosses faithfully in life, we will be ready to place them down at the feet of Christ in death.

Ask yourself:

- *Am I preparing daily for the moment I will entrust my spirit to the Father?*
- *Do I pray for the grace of final perseverance — for myself and for others?*
- *How can I live now in such a way that my death will be a final act of love?*

Closing Prayer

Lord Jesus, grant me the grace of final perseverance. Keep me faithful to Your Cross until my last breath. When my hour comes, receive my spirit into the Father's hands. Let my death be a prayer of love, united to Yours upon the Cross, and open the gates of eternal life.

Amen.

Chapter 41:
The Cross and Eternal Salvation

Reflection – The Price of Our Redemption

At Calvary, Jesus paid the full price for our salvation. No human effort, no act of merit, could open the gates of heaven. Only the Blood of the Lamb, poured out on the Cross, could redeem us.

Eternal salvation is not a reward we earn but a gift we receive — won at a great cost. The Cross is the key that unlocks eternity, the bridge between earth and heaven.

Sheen on Salvation Through the Cross

"There is no salvation apart from the Cross. All who are saved are saved by it — whether they know it or not. The Cross is the one bridge from time to eternity, the one ladder reaching from earth to heaven."

Archbishop Sheen explained that the Cross is not merely a symbol of salvation, but its very source. It is the fountain from which grace flows to every soul.

Illustration – A Soul Saved at the End

A man estranged from the Church for decades received the Sacraments on his deathbed. Holding the crucifix, he whispered: *"This is my passport to heaven."* His final act of faith showed that salvation rests not in our achievements, but in the mercy of Christ crucified.

Invitation – Living in the Light of Salvation

To know that Christ has won eternal life for us should transform how we live. Salvation is already offered; our task is to accept it, live it, and share it with others.

Ask yourself:

- *Do I truly believe that my salvation was purchased on Calvary?*
- *How do I live in gratitude for such a costly gift?*
- *Am I helping others discover the hope of eternal salvation in the Cross?*

Closing Prayer

Saviour of the world, by Your Cross You have redeemed us. I thank You for the gift of eternal life, purchased at such a price. Keep me faithful to Your love, grateful for Your mercy, and eager to share the hope of salvation with others, until I see You face to face in glory.

Amen.

Chapter 42:
The Cross and Eternity

Reflection – The Eternal Sign of Love

The Cross is not only the center of history but the center of eternity. In heaven, the wounds of Christ remain — not as scars of defeat, but as trophies of love. For all eternity, the redeemed will gaze upon the Lamb who was slain and worship the One who loved them unto death.

The Cross reminds us that eternity is not an escape from suffering but the fulfillment of love. What was begun in sacrifice on Calvary will shine forever in glory.

Sheen on the Eternal Cross

"The Cross will never pass away. Time may roll on, empires may crumble, the stars themselves may fade, but the Cross will endure as the eternal proof of God's love. It will be the song of the blessed and the judgment of the lost."

Archbishop Sheen explained that in eternity, the Cross will remain the central mystery — the measure of love and the source of unending joy.

Illustration – A Saint's Vision

St. John, in the Book of Revelation, saw a vision of heaven: the Lamb standing as though slain, surrounded by angels and saints singing: *"Worthy is the Lamb who was slain."* (Revelation 5:12) Eternity is nothing less than the endless contemplation and adoration of Christ crucified and risen.

Invitation – Living for the Eternal Cross

If the Cross is the center of eternity, then it must also be the center of our lives now. To carry our crosses faithfully is to prepare our souls for the unending joy of heaven.

Ask yourself:

- *Do I see my crosses as temporary burdens or as preparations for eternal glory?*
- *Am I learning now to love the Cross, so that I may rejoice in it forever?*
- *How can I live today with my eyes fixed on eternity?*

Closing Prayer

Eternal Lord, Your Cross is my hope on earth and my joy in heaven. Teach me to carry it faithfully now, so that I may adore it eternally with the saints. May the song of my heart echo forever: "Worthy is the Lamb who was slain."

Amen.

Chapter 43: Conclusion: The Cross and the Christian Soul

Reflection – The Soul at Calvary

Every soul stands before the Cross with a choice: to reject it as folly or to embrace it as salvation. The Cross is not only Christ's; it is ours. It marks us, shapes us, and leads us into the mystery of God's love.

To live as a Christian soul is to live in the shadow of Calvary, carrying the Cross daily, trusting in its power, and longing for the glory it promises.

Sheen on the Cross as Personal

"The Cross is not something outside of us. It is within us. We cannot look upon Calvary and say: 'That is His Cross, not mine.' For every Christian soul, the Cross is both burden and blessing, both weight and wing. It is the only way to heaven."

Archbishop Sheen often reminded the faithful that the Cross is not an accessory to Christianity but its essence. Without the Cross, there is no Christ; without Christ, no salvation.

Illustration – A Life Transformed

A young woman once testified: *"When I first looked at the Cross, I saw only suffering. Now I see love. It has changed everything — how I pray, how I forgive, how I live."*

Her journey mirrors that of every soul who learns to see in the Cross not defeat but the face of God's mercy.

Invitation – Making the Cross My Own

The conclusion of every meditation on the Cross is not knowledge but transformation. Each of us is invited to take up our cross and follow Christ, letting it shape our soul into His likeness.

Ask yourself:

- *Do I see the Cross as a distant event, or as the daily pattern of my life?*
- *Am I willing to let the Cross define my identity as a Christian soul?*
- *Will I embrace it not only as burden, but as the greatest gift of love?*

Closing Prayer

Lord Jesus, Your Cross is my salvation and my crown. Engrave it upon my soul, that I may never be separated from it. Teach me to love it, to carry it, to live it, until it leads me home to You. May my soul always rest in the shadow of the Cross, and rise one day in the light of Your Resurrection.

Amen.

Epilogue:
Living the Fruits of the Cross

The Cross does not end with death. It bears fruit in resurrection, in holiness, and in the transformation of those who take it to heart. To meditate on the Seven Last Words is not merely to remember what Christ has done, but to be changed by it — to let the mystery of Calvary shape the way we live each day.

Archbishop Fulton J. Sheen often reminded us that the Cross is not just a place of suffering, but a school of virtue. Each Word spoken from Calvary teaches us how to overcome sin, how to grow in holiness, and how to live the Beatitudes with greater fidelity.

- *"Father, forgive them"* calls us to overcome anger with mercy.
- *"Today you will be with Me in Paradise"* invites us to turn from despair to hope.
- *"Behold your mother"* teaches us to reject isolation and embrace communion with Mary and the Church.

- *"My God, why have You forsaken Me?"* strengthens us to endure desolation with trust.
- *"I thirst"* compels us to overcome indifference with love.
- *"It is finished"* inspires us to persevere in fidelity to our mission.
- *"Father, into Your hands I commit My spirit"* shows us how to die — and how to live — in surrender to God.

The Beatitudes, too, are lived at the foot of the Cross. Poverty of spirit, meekness, hunger for righteousness, purity of heart, mercy, peace, and perseverance in persecution — all of these shine in the Passion of Christ. What He lived perfectly, we are invited to live imperfectly but faithfully.

To practice virtue, then, is not to imitate an abstract ideal but to follow the Crucified One. Each time we choose humility over pride, patience over anger, purity over lust, generosity over selfishness, we are living the fruits of Calvary. Each act of virtue becomes an echo of His sacrifice, a small share in His redemption, a step toward the Beatitudes.

The Cross is not the end of life but the beginning of a new way of living. It is not a burden to be carried alone but a ladder to Heaven, a path of love that transforms us from within. To meditate on the Seven Last Words is to hear Christ's voice speaking into every part of our lives, calling us not just to adore Him, but to follow Him.

May these meditations bear fruit in you. May they strengthen you to practice virtue, to overcome sin, and to live the Beatitudes. And may you, at life's end, be able to say with Christ: *"It is finished."*

Note on the Appendices

The meditations on the Seven Last Words are meant to be prayed, savoured, and lived. Yet prayer does not end with the closing of a book. The Cross continues to guide us into deeper devotion and daily practice.

This appendix has been included not as an afterthought, but as a complement to the meditations contained in this book. Archbishop Fulton J. Sheen often reminded his readers and listeners that the wisdom of the Cross must be lived out in daily life through virtue, prayer, and sacrifice. The materials gathered here — whether they be prayers, reflections, or suggested devotions — are meant to guide the reader from meditation to action, from inspiration to transformation.

In this way, the appendix functions as a bridge: linking Sheen's profound theology with the practical exercises of holiness. It is hoped that those who have prayed and pondered these pages will find in the appendix both a treasury of spiritual helps and an encouragement to persevere in the way of sanctity.

Use them as companions for your prayer, resources for Lent and Holy Week, or as daily reminders that the mystery of the Cross is not only to be contemplated but lived.

Appendix I:
Fulton Sheen on the Seven Last Words

"The Cross is the great pulpit of love. It is here that the drama of the world is played out. The meaning of life, the measure of sin, and the depth of God's mercy are all revealed in those last words." — Fulton J. Sheen

On the First Word – "Father, Forgive Them"

"Forgiveness is the Christlike attitude in the face of injustice. It is not weakness, but strength; not the condoning of evil, but the conquering of it by love."

"Forgiveness is not weakness, but the greatest strength of love. He forgave not because they were innocent, but because love does not wait for repentance to begin its healing."

On the Second Word – "This Day You Will Be with Me in Paradise"

"The thief who stole heaven in the last hour shows us that it is never too late to turn back to God. Mercy is the last appeal of love to the heart of man."

"A dying thief asked for a kingdom, and he received Paradise. No soul that turns to Christ is ever turned away, even in the last hour."

On the Third Word – "Behold Your Mother"

"Mary was not merely the mother of Jesus — she was His masterpiece. He gave her to us because in His wisdom He knew that no one can love Him perfectly who does not love His Mother."

"In giving His Mother to John, Our Lord gave her to us all. She who shared His sufferings now shares in the mission of every Christian life: to bring souls to her Son."

On the Fourth Word – "My God, My God, Why Have You Forsaken Me?"

"There is a difference between feeling abandoned by God and being abandoned by God. He never abandons us. Sometimes He withdraws the awareness of His presence so that we may learn to love Him for Himself, and not for His consolations."

"The cry of abandonment was not despair but solidarity. He entered into the loneliness of every human heart, so that no one would ever suffer alone."

On the Fifth Word – "I Thirst"

"His thirst is for souls, not for water. Our Lord is more anxious for our salvation than we are ourselves. He is like a shepherd who cannot rest while one sheep is lost."

"When Our Lord said, 'I thirst,' He revealed His longing for souls. He thirsts for our love, our repentance, our prayers. Only when we give Him ourselves is His thirst consoled."

On the Sixth Word – "It Is Finished"

"It was not the cry of one who was broken, but of one who had broken through. The Cross was His goal, not His fate. Having drained the cup of suffering, He handed it back empty to the Father."

"Christ did not say, 'I am finished,' but 'It is finished.' He proclaimed His mission accomplished, His sacrifice complete, His work of redemption done."

On the Seventh Word – "Father, Into Your Hands I Commit My Spirit"

"Our Lord teaches us how to die – with our hearts in the hands of the Father. Life becomes complete not when we hold on, but when we let go into His love."

"The final act of Our Lord was an act of trust. As He gave His Spirit into the Father's hands, He showed us how to live – and how to die – in surrender to God."

Appendix II:
Prayers Before the Crucifix

Prayer of St. Francis of Assisi

Most High, glorious God, enlighten the darkness of my heart.

Give me right faith, sure hope, and perfect charity.

Grant me understanding and knowledge, Lord,

that I may carry out Your holy and true command. Amen.

The Anima Christi

Soul of Christ, sanctify me.

Body of Christ, save me.

Blood of Christ, inebriate me.

Water from the side of Christ, wash me.

Passion of Christ, strengthen me.

O good Jesus, hear me.

Within Your wounds, hide me.

Separated from You, let me never be.

From the evil one, protect me.

At the hour of my death, call me.

And bid me come to You,

that with Your saints I may praise You

forever and ever.

Amen.

Prayer Before a Crucifix

Behold, O kind and most sweet Jesus,

I cast myself upon my knees in Your sight,

and with the most fervent desire of my soul,

I pray and beseech You to imprint upon my heart

lively sentiments of faith, hope, and charity,

with true contrition for my sins, and a firm

purpose of amendment.

While with deep affection and grief of soul I

ponder within myself

and mentally contemplate Your five wounds,

having before my eyes that which David spoke in prophecy of You, O good Jesus:

"They have pierced my hands and my feet; they have numbered all my bones."

Sheen's Meditation Before the Cross

"Kneel at the Cross, and you will find yourself taller than the world.

Look upon His wounds, and your wounds will find their healing.

Lay your burdens there, and you will rise lighter than when you came."

Prayer of Surrender at Calvary
(Inspired by the Seventh Word)

Father, into Your hands I commit my spirit.

Into Your hands I place my life,

my family, my work, my joys, and my sorrows.

Into Your hands I place my fears and my hopes,

my health and my future.

Into Your hands I place my sins,

trusting in Your mercy.

Hold me close to Your heart,

now and at the hour of my death.

Amen.

Appendix III:
Stations of the Cross

These meditations are adapted in the spirit of Fulton J. Sheen, who called the Cross the "university of love."

Short Meditations for The Stations of the Cross

1. Jesus is Condemned to Death

O Jesus, though innocent, You accepted condemnation. Teach me to accept injustice with patience, and to unite it with Your sacrifice.

2. Jesus Takes Up His Cross

Lord, You embraced Your Cross willingly. Help me to embrace my daily crosses with love, instead of complaint.

3. Jesus Falls the First Time

Weakened and crushed, You stumbled under the Cross. Lift me when I fall into sin, and grant me perseverance.

4. Jesus Meets His Mother

Mary, sharing His sorrow, strengthens Him with her presence. Teach me to turn to Our Lady in every trial.

5. Simon Helps Jesus Carry His Cross

Lord, You allowed Simon to share Your burden. Teach me to help others with their crosses and to see You in them.

6. Veronica Wipes the Face of Jesus

Lord, she gave You comfort with a simple act of love. Teach me that no act of charity is ever forgotten by You.

7. Jesus Falls the Second Time

You fell again, exhausted by the weight of sin. Lift me up whenever I grow weary in the struggle for holiness.

8. Jesus Consoles the Women of Jerusalem

Even in suffering, You consoled others. Help me to comfort those around me, even in my own trials.

9. Jesus Falls the Third Time

O Lord, crushed to the ground, You rose once more. Grant me perseverance to rise each time I fall.

10. Jesus is Stripped of His Garments

Deprived of all dignity, You accepted humiliation. Clothe me in humility and purity of heart.

11. Jesus is Nailed to the Cross

The nails fastened You to the wood, but it was love that held You there. Teach me to be faithful in sacrifice.

12. Jesus Dies on the Cross

Lord, in Your final surrender, You redeemed the world. May my last breath be one of trust in You.

13. Jesus is Taken Down from the Cross

Your lifeless body rested in Mary's arms. Teach me to find comfort in her maternal embrace.

14. Jesus is Laid in the Tomb

In silence You rested, awaiting resurrection. Teach me to hope in Your promises beyond every darkness.

Stations of the Cross

Opening Prayer

Lord Jesus, as I walk with You on the road to Calvary, open my heart to see in each step the depth of Your love. Teach me to unite my crosses with Yours, so that my life may be transformed in Your service. Amen.

First Station – Jesus is Condemned to Death
Lord, You stood before the judgment seat, silent before false accusations. Teach me to accept misunderstanding without bitterness, offering it for love of You.

Second Station – Jesus Takes Up His Cross
You embraced the wood that would save the world. Help me to take up my own daily cross, seeing it not as punishment but as a path to glory.

Third Station – Jesus Falls the First Time
Your body was weak, but Your love was strong. When I fall under the weight of my sins, lift me up in Your mercy.

Fourth Station – Jesus Meets His Blessed Mother
Her eyes met Yours, and her heart shared Your pain. Teach me to find in Mary the strength to endure my own sorrows with grace.

Fifth Station – Simon of Cyrene Helps Jesus Carry the Cross
Lord, You allowed another to share Your burden. Help me to accept help from others, and to offer my help freely when I see another's need.

Sixth Station – Veronica Wipes the Face of Jesus
She braved the crowd to comfort You. Give me the courage to show kindness even when the world mocks or turns away.

Seventh Station – Jesus Falls the Second Time
Lord, You rose again after a second fall. When I am weary from repeated failure, give me the grace to keep going.

Eighth Station – Jesus Comforts the Women of Jerusalem
Even in agony, You thought of others. Teach me to speak hope into the lives of those who mourn.

Ninth Station – Jesus Falls the Third Time
Crushed to the ground, You did not stay there. Help me to rise again when life has knocked me flat.

Tenth Station – Jesus is Stripped of His Garments
You accepted humiliation without resentment. Free me from attachment to possessions and appearances, so that my worth may be found only in You.

Eleventh Station – Jesus is Nailed to the Cross
Lord, each blow of the hammer was for my salvation. Let me never take Your sacrifice for granted.

Twelfth Station – Jesus Dies on the Cross
From the Cross, You forgave, You thirsted, You surrendered. Teach me to die to self so that I may live in You.

Thirteenth Station – Jesus is Taken Down from the Cross
Mary cradled Your lifeless body. Teach me to hold others in their pain with tenderness and faith.

Fourteenth Station – Jesus is Laid in the Tomb
The world thought it was over, but Heaven knew otherwise. Help me to trust in Your plan, even when I see only darkness.

Closing Prayer
Lord Jesus, thank You for walking this way for love of me. May I never forget the price You paid for my redemption, and may my life be a constant "yes" to Your call. Amen.

Appendix IV: Suggested Scriptures for Meditation on the Passion

From the Gospels

- Matthew 26–27: The Passion according to Matthew
- Mark 14–15: The Passion according to Mark
- Luke 22–23: The Passion according to Luke
- John 18–19: The Passion according to John
-

From the Prophets and Psalms

- Isaiah 52:13–53:12: The Suffering Servant
- Psalm 22: The Psalm of the Forsaken One
- Lamentations 1–3: The Sorrow of Jerusalem
- Zechariah 12:10: They shall look on Him whom they pierced

From the Epistles

- Philippians 2:5-11: Christ's Humility and Exaltation
- Hebrews 5:7-9: Christ's Obedience through Suffering
- 1 Peter 2:21-25: Christ's Suffering as an Example

Prophecies of the Passion *(Old Testament)*

- **Isaiah 50:4-11** – The Suffering Servant's obedience.
- **Isaiah 52:13 – 53:12** – The Man of Sorrows.
- **Psalm 22** – My God, my God, why have You forsaken me?
- **Psalm 69:1-21** – Zeal for Your house consumes me.
- **Wisdom 2:12-24** – The plotting against the righteous one.
- **Zechariah 12:10 – 13:1** – They shall look upon Him whom they have pierced.

The Last Supper and Gethsemane

- **Luke 22:14-38** – The Last Supper and institution of the Eucharist.
- **John 13:1-17** – Jesus washes the disciples' feet.
- **John 15:9-17** – Abide in My love.
- **Matthew 26:36-46** – The agony in the garden.
- **Luke 22:39-46** – Father, if You are willing…
- **Hebrews 5:7-9** – He learned obedience through suffering.

The Trial and Condemnation

- **Matthew 26:57-68** – Jesus before the high priest.
- **Luke 22:63-71** – Jesus is mocked and beaten.
- **John 18:28-40** – Jesus before Pilate.
- **John 19:1-16** – Ecce Homo – Behold the Man.
- **Isaiah 53:7** – Like a lamb before its shearers is silent.

The Way of the Cross

- **Luke 23:26–31** – Simon of Cyrene and the daughters of Jerusalem.
- **Mark 15:21–32** – The soldiers mock Him.
- **Matthew 27:32–44** – The crucifixion.
- **John 19:17–24** – They divided My garments among them.
- **Philippians 2:5–11** – He humbled Himself unto death, even death on a cross.

The Seven Last Words *(Gospel References)*

1. **Luke 23:34** – Father, forgive them.
2. **Luke 23:43** – Today you will be with Me in paradise.
3. **John 19:26–27** – Behold your mother.
4. **Matthew 27:46** – My God, my God, why have You forsaken Me?
5. **John 19:28** – I thirst.
6. **John 19:30** – It is finished.
7. **Luke 23:46** – Father, into Your hands I commit My spirit.

Death and Burial of Jesus

- **Matthew 27:45–56** – The death of Jesus.
- **John 19:31–42** – The piercing of His side and burial.
- **Luke 23:50–56** – The burial by Joseph of Arimathea.
- **Isaiah 53:9** – He was with a rich man in His death.

Suggested Use:

- **Lenten Devotion:** Meditate on one passage daily.
- **Holy Week:** Read the Passion narratives in sequence.
- **Holy Hour:** Choose one or two passages and remain with them in silence before the Crucifix or the Blessed Sacrament.

Appendix V:
Hymns and Chants of the Passion

Stabat Mater Dolorosa

(Traditionally sung during the Stations of the Cross - Full text may be prayed in Latin or in English translation.)

1   At the cross her station keeping,

     Stood the mournful Mother weeping,

     Close to Jesus to the last.

2   Through her heart, his sorrow sharing,

     All his bitter anguish bearing,

     Now at length the sword has passed.

3   O how sad and sore distressed,

     Was that Mother highly blest

     Of the sole begotten One!

4   Christ above in torment hangs,
        She beneath beholds the pangs
        Of her dying, glorious Son.

5   Is there one who would not weep,
        Whelmed in miseries so deep,
        Christ's dear Mother to behold?

6   Can the human heart refrain
        From partaking in her pain,
        In that Mother's pain untold?

7   Bruised, derided, cursed, defiled,
        She beheld her tender Child,
        All with bloody scourges rent.

8   For the sins of his own nation
        Saw him hang in desolation
        Till his spirit forth he sent.

9   O thou Mother! Font of love,
Touch my spirit from above,
Make my heart with thine accord.

10   Make me feel as thou hast felt;
Make my soul to glow and melt
With the love of Christ, my Lord.

11   Holy Mother, pierce me through,
In my heart each wound renew
Of my Savior crucified.

12   Let me share with thee His pain,
Who for all my sins was slain,
Who for me in torment died.

13   Let me mingle tears with thee,
Mourning Him who mourned for me,
All the days that I may live.

14   By the cross with thee to stay;

        There with thee to weep and pray,

        All I ask of thee to give.

15   Virgin of all Virgins best!

        Listen to my fond request:

        Let me share thy grief divine.

O Sacred Head Surrounded

O sacred Head surrounded
By crown of piercing thorn!
O bleeding Head, so wounded,
Reviled and put to scorn!
The pow'r of death comes o'er you,
The glow of life decays,
Yet angel hosts adore you
And tremble as they gaze.

I see your strength and vigor
All fading in the strife,
And death with cruel rigor,
Bereaving you of life;
O agony and dying!
O love to sinners free!
Jesus, all grace supplying,
O turn your face on me.

In this, your bitter passion,
Good Shepherd, think of me
With your most sweet compassion,
Unworthy though I be:
Beneath your cross abiding
Forever would I rest,
In your dear love confiding,

Pange Lingua Gloriosi *(English)*

(Down in Adoration Falling)

1. Sing, my tongue, the Saviour's glory,
   Of His Flesh, the mystery sing;
   Of the Blood, all price exceeding,
   Shed by our Immortal King,
   Destined, for the world's redemption,
   From a noble Womb to spring.

2. Of a pure and spotless Virgin
   Born for us on earth below,
   He, as Man, with man conversing,
   Stayed, the seeds of truth to sow;
   Then He closed in solemn order
   Wondrously His Life of woe.

3. On the night of that Last Supper,
   Seated with His chosen band,
   He, the Paschal Victim eating,
   First fulfils the Law's command;
   Then as Food to all his brethren
   Gives Himself with His own Hand.

4. Word-made-Flesh, the bread of nature
By His Word to Flesh He turns;
Wine into His Blood He changes:
What though sense no change discerns,
Only be the heart in earnest,
Faith her lesson quickly learns.

5. Down in adoration falling,
Lo, the sacred Host we hail,
Lo, o'er ancient forms departing,
Newer rites of grace prevail;
Faith for all defects supplying,
When the feeble senses fail.

6. To the Everlasting Father,
And the Son who comes on high,
With the Holy Ghost proceeding,
Forth from each eternally,
Be salvation, honor, blessing,
Might and endless majesty.

Amen.

Liturgical Note

Many of these hymns are traditionally sung during **Lent**, **Holy Week**, and particularly during the **Stations of the Cross**, **Good Friday Liturgy**, and **Adoration of the Cross**.

Including the Latin allows for those who wish to sing or pray them in the Church's heritage language, while the English translation makes them accessible for personal devotion.

Appendix VI: Guide to Making a Holy Hour at Calvary

Archbishop Fulton J. Sheen called the daily Holy Hour the "hour of power." For over sixty years of priesthood, he spent one hour each day before the Blessed Sacrament, drawing strength for his preaching and intimacy for his soul. He urged every Christian to do the same.

This guide is offered to help you enter into prayer at the foot of the Cross, uniting your Holy Hour to Calvary.

1. Begin in Silence

Kneel before the crucifix or the Blessed Sacrament. Make an act of adoration and recollection.

2. Read from Scripture

Choose a passage from the Passion (Matthew 26–27, Mark 14–15, Luke 22–23, or John

18-19). Let the words draw you into Christ's suffering love.

3. Meditate on the Seven Last Words

Take one Word at a time, recalling the meditations in this book. Pause to reflect on how it applies to your own life and how you can make reparation.

4. Pray with Mary

Pray the Rosary or a Marian hymn, standing with Our Lady at the foot of the Cross. Ask her to help you share in her fidelity and compassion.

5. Offer Reparation

Bring before Christ the sins of the world — your own, those of your family, the Church, and all humanity. Whisper acts of love to console His Sacred Heart.

8. Rest in His Presence

Allow silence to speak. Listen. Offer your heart. Remember Sheen's words: *"The greatest love story of all time is contained in a tiny white Host."*

9. **Conclude with Thanksgiving**

End with a prayer of gratitude for the gift of the Cross. Ask for the grace to carry your daily crosses in union with His.

Practical Note: Even if you cannot make a full sixty minutes, begin with what you can. Ten, fifteen, or thirty minutes of faithful prayer will bear fruit if offered with love.

Guide to Making a Holy Hour at Calvary

Purpose of the Holy Hour
The Holy Hour is an invitation to watch and pray with Jesus in His Passion, uniting ourselves with Him at Calvary. Archbishop Fulton Sheen made a daily Holy Hour for over 60 years, calling it the "hour of power" in his life and ministry.

Preparation
Choose a quiet place: before the Blessed Sacrament, in an Adoration Chapel, or before a crucifix at home.
Silence your phone and set aside distractions.
Ask the Holy Spirit to help you enter deeply into the mystery of the Cross.

Suggested Structure for the Hour

1. Opening Prayer (2–3 minutes)
Begin with a prayer inviting the Lord to be with you: Lord Jesus, I come to be with You in this hour. You are my crucified King, my Savior, my Friend. Teach me to love You as You have loved me. Amen.

2. Scripture Reading (5–7 minutes)
Read one of the Passion narratives:
Matthew 26–27
Mark 14–15
Luke 22–23
John 18–19
Pause and let a word or phrase remain in your heart.

3. Meditation on the Seven Last Words (15–20 minutes)
Reflect on each Word slowly. You may use the meditations from *The Cross and the Last Words* or another source.
Pause after each Word to speak to the Lord from your heart.

4. Intercessory Prayer (10 minutes)
At the foot of the Cross, place before Jesus:
Your own needs.
The needs of loved ones.
The needs of the Church and the world.

5. Contemplative Silence (10 minutes)
Simply remain with Him.
Gaze upon the Crucifix or the Blessed Sacrament, aware of His love and presence.

6. Concluding Act of Surrender (5 minutes)
Pray in your own words, or use this act of entrustment:
Father, into Your hands I commit my spirit,
my heart, my past, my present, my future.
May Your will be done in me,
as it was in Jesus at Calvary.
Amen.

Additional Practices
Pray the Stations of the Cross during the hour.
Sing or pray a Passion hymn.
Write a short letter to Jesus expressing your love and gratitude.

Encouragement from Fulton Sheen:
"The purpose of the Holy Hour is not to change God, but to change us. It is to conform our lives to the will of Him who loved us to the end."

Appendix VII:
Overcoming Sin, Practicing Virtue, and Living the Beatitudes

Introduction

The Seven Last Words of Christ are more than a record of what Christ said before dying. They are the living voice of God addressing every generation, every heart, and every struggle. Archbishop Fulton J. Sheen returned again and again to these words throughout his preaching, because he recognized in them the perfect summary of the Christian life.

Archbishop Fulton J. Sheen said: *"Unless souls are saved, nothing is saved."* The Cross was His mission of salvation; our share in it is to let grace transform us into saints.

In three of his classic works — *Victory over Vice,* *The Seven Virtues,* and *The Cross and the Beatitudes* — Sheen showed how each Word of the Crucified Christ provides a remedy for sin, a lesson in virtue, and a living portrait of the

Beatitudes. At Calvary, Christ not only saves us; He also shows us how to live.

What follows is a synthesis of Sheen's insights. It is a spiritual roadmap: first, how to **overcome sin**; second, how to **practice virtue**; and third, how to **live the Beatitudes**.

Overcoming Sin

At the Cross, sin is unmasked and defeated. Pride is conquered by humility, anger by forgiveness, lust by purity, envy by gratitude, sloth by perseverance, greed by generosity, gluttony by fasting and self-denial. Each vice finds its antidote in the Passion of Christ.

Sheen's Insight:

"Our Lord did not die to remove suffering, but to give meaning to it. Each word from the Cross not only redeems but also heals the wounds sin has left in us."

Sheen's Wisdom:

"The Cross is not an accident in life, but the answer to sin. Each word from Calvary is a medicine — bitter perhaps, but healing for the soul."

Practicing Virtue

Every virtue is a share in the life of Christ:

- **Fortitude** endures trials with patience.
- **Hope** looks to Paradise, as the Good Thief did.
- **Prudence** chooses rightly in the light of the Cross.
- **Faith** clings to God in darkness, as He did in His cry of abandonment.
- **Temperance** disciplines desire.
- **Justice** gives to God and neighbor what is their due.
- **Charity** forgives, thirsts, and loves without limit.

Sheen's Insight:

"Virtue is not mere avoidance of sin, but the blossoming of love. At Calvary, Christ shows us that the highest virtue is to give oneself completely."

Sheen's Wisdom:

"Virtue is not repression but transformation. Calvary shows us not what to avoid, but what to become."

Living the Beatitudes

The Beatitudes are not lofty ideals but the very shape of Calvary:

- Meekness: His silence before accusers.
- Mercy: His forgiveness of His enemies.
- Purity of heart: His undivided will to the Father.
- Poor in spirit: Christ who emptied Himself.
- Hunger for righteousness: His thirst for souls.
- Peacemaking: His reconciling of Heaven and earth.
- Mourning: Mary and the faithful who grieved with Him.

- Persecution for righteousness: His Cross itself.

To live the Beatitudes is to live beneath the Cross — humble, meek, merciful, pure, steadfast, and faithful unto death.

Sheen's Insight:

"The Beatitudes are Christ's autobiography. On the Cross, they are not preached but lived."

Sheen's Wisdom:

"The Beatitudes are not ideals to admire but laws to live. On Calvary, they are not preached but practiced."

Conclusion

The Cross is not only our redemption but our pattern of life. Practicing virtue, overcoming sin, and living the Beatitudes are the fruits of Calvary. They are the way we turn meditation into action, prayer into witness, and faith into love.

At the Cross, Christ conquers sin, perfects virtue, and embodies the Beatitudes. His Seven Last Words are not only His farewell gift to the world, but also a practical guide for our sanctification.

To stand beneath the Cross is to enter the school of Christ. Here we learn how to overcome vice, how to practice virtue, and how to live the Beatitudes — not in theory, but in the flesh, in daily life, in love poured out.

As Archbishop Sheen said: *"The Cross is not something to be escaped; it is something to be embraced. It is the key, not only to heaven, but to happiness here on earth."*

Introduction to Reflections on Overcoming Sin, Practicing Virtue, and Living the Beatitudes

The meditations you have just read invite you to stand at Calvary, listening to the Seven Last Words of Christ and discovering their power for the Christian soul. These final reflections, gathered here as an appendix, continue that same pilgrimage — but with a shift of focus.

Here we move from the mystery of the Cross itself to its practical fruit in daily life: overcoming sin, cultivating virtue, and embracing the Beatitudes. Archbishop Fulton Sheen often reminded us that the Passion of Christ is not merely to be admired but to be imitated. To gaze upon the Crucified is to be invited into conversion, renewal, and holiness.

This section is placed at the end of the book deliberately. Not all readers may feel ready to take up these demanding meditations right away. They are offered as a companion guide for those who wish to go further, who wish to let the Cross shape not only their prayer but their way of living.

Whether read immediately or returned to later, these reflections are meant to be a **practical school of discipleship**, showing how the victory of Calvary takes root in our own lives.

Part I
Overcoming Sin

Introduction

Before we can live fully in the grace of the Cross, we must first face the reality of sin. Archbishop Fulton Sheen often reminded us that sin is not simply the breaking of a law but the wounding of love — the rejection of God's friendship. At Calvary, Christ bore every sin in His own Body so that we might be free.

These reflections are not meant to discourage, but to liberate. By naming the sins that so often enslave the human heart, we can learn to place them beneath the Cross and discover there the mercy that heals and restores.

- Reflection 1 – Overcoming the Sin of Anger
- Reflection 2 – Overcoming the Sin of Envy
- Reflection 3 – Overcoming the Sin of Lust
- Reflection 4 – Overcoming the Sin of Pride
- Reflection 5 – Overcoming the Sin of Gluttony
- Reflection 6 – Overcoming the Sin of Sloth
- Reflection 7 – Overcoming the Sin of Greed

Reflection 1:
Overcoming the Sin of Anger

The First Word: *"Father, forgive them, for they know not what they do."*

Reflection – Anger Healed by Forgiveness

Anger burns hot when we feel wronged, betrayed, or humiliated. It demands vengeance, clings to resentment, and refuses peace. Yet the Cross reveals a new path: when Jesus was mocked, scourged, and crucified, He did not curse His enemies — He forgave them.

The true antidote to anger is not suppression, but transformation. In forgiving, Christ shows us that anger is conquered by mercy.

Sheen on Anger in the First Word

"Anger is love of justice perverted to revenge. Our Lord satisfied justice not by punishing, but by forgiving. The cure for anger is forgiveness — not once, but seventy times seven."

Archbishop Sheen taught that anger wastes its fire on destruction, while Christ's fire of love transforms pain into peace.

Illustration – The Power of Forgiveness

A man whose son was killed by violence stunned the courtroom by telling the offender: *"I forgive you. I will pray for you."* That act broke the cycle of hate. His courage revealed that forgiveness disarms anger more powerfully than retaliation ever could.

Invitation – Letting Go of Wrath

To overcome anger, we must release our claim to vengeance and hand it over to God. Forgiveness does not mean forgetting the wrong, but choosing not to let anger rule our hearts.

Ask yourself:

- *Do I allow anger to poison my thoughts and words?*
- *Who is God asking me to forgive today?*
- *Am I willing to surrender my anger to the Cross, where love has the last word?*

Closing Prayer

Lord Jesus, You answered anger with forgiveness. Take from me the poison of wrath, the chains of resentment, and the desire for revenge. Teach me to forgive as You forgave, so that anger may give way to peace.

Amen.

Reflection 2:
Overcoming the Sin of Envy

The Second Word: *"This day you will be with Me in Paradise."*

Reflection – Envy Healed by Trust in Mercy

Envy looks at the blessings of others with resentment, as if God's generosity to them were an injustice to us. At Calvary, two thieves hung beside Jesus. One mocked Him, resentful even in death; the other humbled himself, asking only to be remembered.

In a single moment, envy was conquered by trust. The good thief discovered that God's mercy is never diminished by being shared — there is room in paradise for all.

Sheen on Envy in the Second Word

"Envy is sadness at another's good. The cure is to fix our eyes not on what others receive, but on Christ. One thief looked at Jesus with envy, the other with hope — and one was lost, the other saved."

Archbishop Sheen showed that envy shrivels the soul, while gratitude and trust in mercy open it wide to heaven.

Illustration – The Joy of Another's Blessing

A young woman unable to conceive struggled with jealousy of her sister, who had children. At last, she began to pray not for her own blessing, but for joy in her sister's gift. To her surprise, peace entered her heart. Her envy gave way to gratitude, and she discovered freedom in celebrating another's good.

Invitation – Rejoicing in God's Generosity

To overcome envy, we must see life as gift. God's mercy is abundant, not scarce. The blessings of others are not threats, but reminders that God is generous to all.

Ask yourself:

- *Do I resent the blessings others receive?*
- *Can I learn to thank God for gifts He gives to my neighbor?*
- *Am I able to trust that He has a place in paradise prepared also for me?*

Closing Prayer

Lord Jesus,
You promised paradise to the repentant thief.
Take envy from my heart,
and teach me to rejoice in the good of others.
Help me to trust in Your mercy,
confident that Your blessings are without limit.
Amen.

Reflection 3:
Overcoming the Sin of Lust

The Third Word: *"Behold your Mother."*

Reflection – Lust Healed by Purity of Love

Lust is the distortion of love into self-gratification, seeking pleasure without sacrifice. At Calvary, Jesus revealed the opposite: love that gives, not takes. In entrusting Mary to John and John to Mary, Christ established a new family of pure, selfless love.

The remedy to lust is not repression but transformation — learning to love with reverence, purity, and responsibility.

Sheen on Lust in the Third Word

"Lust looks upon others as objects; Christ looked upon His Mother and John as souls. Lust takes; love gives. Purity is not the absence of passion but the right ordering of it toward sacrifice."

Archbishop Sheen taught that true purity is not weakness but strength: the discipline that makes love self-giving rather than self-seeking.

Illustration – Chastity as Love's Strength

A young couple once decided to live chastely before marriage. They admitted it was difficult but later said: *"Our love was purified by sacrifice. We gave each other respect before we gave our bodies."* Their story shows how purity prepares the heart for enduring love.

Invitation – Seeing with Pure Eyes

To overcome lust, we must see every person as Christ sees them — not as objects of desire but as children of God. Purity frees the heart to love rightly and deeply.

Ask yourself:

- *Do I treat others as objects of pleasure or as persons to be cherished?*
- *Am I willing to sacrifice comfort for purity of heart?*
- *Do I invite Mary, Mother most pure, into my struggles against lust?*

Closing Prayer

Lord Jesus, on the Cross You gave us Your Mother. Through her intercession, purify my heart and heal my desires. Teach me to love with reverence, to see others with pure eyes, and to make my life a gift of love.

Amen.

Reflection 4:
Overcoming the Sin of Pride

The Fourth Word: *"My God, My God, why have You forsaken Me?"*

Reflection – Pride Healed by Humble Faith

Pride is the root of all sin — the refusal to depend on God, the illusion that we are self-sufficient. On Calvary, Jesus embraced the very opposite: in His cry of abandonment, He showed total dependence on the Father, even when He felt nothing but silence.

The cure for pride is humility — admitting our weakness and trusting God even when we do not understand.

Sheen on Pride in the Fourth Word

"Pride says, 'I will not serve.' On the Cross, Christ showed the humility of the obedient Son. His cry was not despair but faith, clinging to the Father when the Father seemed absent."

Archbishop Sheen explained that Christ dismantled pride by embracing radical humility — obedience unto death.

Illustration – Humility in Trial

A successful businessman lost everything in an economic collapse. At first, pride raged: *"How could this happen to me?"* Yet, slowly, he learned to pray: *"Into Your hands, Lord."* In losing his pride, he discovered deeper trust in God's providence.

Invitation – Living Humility

To overcome pride, we must embrace dependence on God, acknowledging that every breath is His gift. Humility is not weakness but strength: the courage to let God be God.

Ask yourself:

- *Do I rely on myself more than on God?*
- *Am I willing to surrender my pride and accept my dependence on Him?*
- *How can I grow in humility through obedience, patience, and trust?*

Closing Prayer

My God, when pride tempts me to rely on myself, teach me humility. When You seem silent, grant me faith to cling to You still. May I never exalt myself, but always find strength in surrender.

Amen.

Reflection 5:
Overcoming the Sin of Gluttony

The Fifth Word: *"I thirst."*

Reflection – Gluttony Healed by Holy Desire

Gluttony is the disordered craving for pleasure, especially in food and drink, but also in anything that dulls the soul with excess. On the Cross, Jesus revealed the deepest hunger and thirst of the human heart: not for excess, but for God.

His cry, *"I thirst,"* was more than physical. It was a thirst for righteousness, for souls, for the Father's will. Gluttony enslaves; holy desire frees.

Sheen on Gluttony in the Fifth Word

"When Our Lord said, 'I thirst,' He lifted desire to its highest level. Gluttony makes the stomach a god; Christ makes God our only satisfaction. The cure for gluttony is to hunger and thirst for justice."

Archbishop Sheen emphasized that Jesus teaches us to redirect our appetites — from indulgence to sacrifice, from excess to holiness.

Illustration – Choosing the Higher Hunger

During Lent, a young man gave up alcohol, not just to deny himself but to replace the craving with prayer. He discovered that every time he resisted, his heart grew freer. His small sacrifice reminded him of Christ's thirst for souls.

Invitation – Purifying My Appetites

To overcome gluttony, we must discipline our desires, moderating what is good and rejecting what enslaves. True satisfaction is not in abundance but in God alone.

Ask yourself:

- *Do I allow food, drink, or comfort to master me?*
- *Am I willing to fast or sacrifice to discipline my appetites?*
- *Do I thirst more for pleasure or for God's love?*

Closing Prayer

O Jesus, who thirsted for souls upon the Cross, purify my desires. Teach me to hunger for righteousness, to thirst for holiness, and to find my true satisfaction in You alone.

Amen.

Reflection 6:
Overcoming the Sin of Sloth

The Sixth Word: *"It is finished."*

Reflection – Sloth Healed by Perseverance

Sloth is more than laziness; it is the refusal of effort in the spiritual life, the indifference to love's demands. On Calvary, Jesus declared: *"It is finished."* He did not abandon His mission halfway, but completed it in perfect fidelity.

Sloth withers the soul by keeping it lukewarm. The Cross ignites zeal by showing that love perseveres until the end.

Sheen on Sloth in the Sixth Word

"Sloth is not the love of ease, but the refusal of sacrifice. It is the sadness of the soul that will not strive for the highest. Our Lord conquered sloth by completing the work the Father gave Him to do."

Archbishop Sheen taught that Christ's triumph over sloth calls us to wholehearted dedication in the duties of our state in life.

Illustration – Perseverance in Duty

A nurse caring for the dying once admitted: *"There are days I want to quit. But then I look at the crucifix and remember: He finished His work. I must finish mine."* Her fidelity transformed her weariness into love.

Invitation – Finishing the Work Entrusted to Me

To overcome sloth, we must embrace diligence in prayer, work, and love. Even small duties become holy when done with perseverance.

Ask yourself:

- *Am I neglecting prayer or duty out of laziness or indifference?*
- *Do I abandon commitments when they grow difficult?*
- *How can I persevere like Christ, completing the tasks given to me?*

Closing Prayer

Lord Jesus, You conquered sloth by finishing the work of redemption. Grant me zeal in prayer, diligence in duty, and perseverance in love. Let me not grow weary, but bring to completion the mission You entrust to me.

Amen.

Reflection 7:
Overcoming the Sin of Greed

The Seventh Word: *"Father, into Your hands I commend My spirit."*

Reflection – Greed Healed by Surrender

Greed clings tightly to possessions, power, and control, seeking security in what cannot last. On the Cross, Jesus did the opposite: He let go of everything — His strength, His breath, His very life — and placed it all into the Father's hands.

The cure for greed is generosity: surrendering our lives, goods, and hearts into God's keeping. Only when we let go do we discover true freedom.

Sheen on Greed in the Seventh Word

"Greed seeks to grasp; Christ chose to give. Greed hoards; Christ surrendered. In His final word, He placed everything in the Father's hands — teaching us that the only wealth worth keeping is the wealth of love."

Archbishop Sheen explained that greed shrinks the soul, but surrender expands it into eternity.

Illustration – Letting Go in Faith

A wealthy man once sold his possessions to fund missions overseas. When asked why, he said: *"I cannot take them with me, but I can send them ahead."* His surrender turned earthly wealth into eternal treasure.

Invitation – Living Generously

To overcome greed, we must practice detachment: using possessions without being possessed by them, and living with open hands before God.

Ask yourself:

- *Do I cling too tightly to money, status, or security?*
- *Am I willing to let go, trusting God as my true treasure?*
- *How can I practice generosity today in imitation of Christ's surrender?*

Closing Prayer

Father of Mercy, into Your hands I commend my spirit. Free me from greed and grasping, teach me to live with open hands, and let my wealth be found in love. May I surrender all I have and am to You, as Christ did upon the Cross.

Amen.

Part II – Practicing Virtue

Introduction

The Cross does more than free us from sin; it strengthens us to grow in virtue. Every nail, every wound, every word of Christ on Calvary is an invitation to live differently — to embody faith, hope, charity, and the other virtues that make us sons and daughters of God.

Archbishop Sheen often taught that holiness is not a single heroic act, but a habit of daily fidelity. Virtue is the steady flame that burns in the soul, even in the darkness. These meditations will help us see how the grace of the Cross can shape our thoughts, our actions, and our character, until Christ Himself is formed within us.

- Reflection 1 – Practicing the Virtue of Fortitude
- Reflection 2 – Practicing the Virtue of Hope
- Reflection 3 – Practicing the Virtue of Prudence
- Reflection 4 – Practicing the Virtue of Faith
- Reflection 5 – Practicing the Virtue of Temperance
- Reflection 6 – Practicing the Virtue of Justice
- Reflection 7 – Practicing the Virtue of Charity

Reflection 1:
Practicing the Virtue of Fortitude

The First Word: *"Father, forgive them, for they know not what they do."*

Reflection – Courage in the Face of Injustice

Fortitude is not the absence of fear but the strength to remain faithful in the face of suffering. On Calvary, Jesus demonstrated fortitude not by striking back at His enemies but by forgiving them. True courage is not retaliation, but endurance rooted in love.

To forgive in the midst of pain requires a heroism greater than violence. The Cross teaches us that fortitude is the power to face hatred without losing charity.

Sheen on Fortitude in the First Word

"The true courage of Christ was not in avoiding the Cross but in mounting it. Not in calling down fire upon His enemies, but in forgiving them. Fortitude is not the defiance of pain, but the endurance of it for love's sake."

Archbishop Sheen saw fortitude as the foundation of the Christian life. Without it, every other virtue collapses under trial.

Illustration – A Martyr's Courage

St. Stephen, the first martyr, echoed the words of Christ: *"Lord, do not hold this sin against them."* (Acts 7:60) In his moment of death, Stephen revealed the fortitude of the Cross — courage not to curse his killers, but to bless them.

This same spirit is possible in our lives, in smaller sacrifices, when we respond to injustice with patience and love.

Invitation – Learning Courage in Forgiveness

Fortitude is not only for martyrs. It is for parents enduring hardship, workers facing ridicule, the sick bearing pain, and every Christian asked to forgive. To practice fortitude is to stand firm at Calvary with Christ.

Ask yourself:

- *Do I meet trials with courage, or with resentment?*
- *Can I forgive those who wrong me, even when it costs me dearly?*
- *Am I willing to be strong not by striking back, but by enduring in love?*
-

Closing Prayer

Lord Jesus, You showed fortitude on the Cross by forgiving Your enemies in love. Grant me courage to face my trials, strength to endure my sufferings, and the grace to forgive as You forgave. Let me be strong not in anger, but in mercy.

Amen.

Reflection 2:
Practicing the Virtue of Hope

The Second Word: *"This day you will be with Me in paradise."*

Reflection – Hope in the Face of Death

Hope looks beyond the present suffering to the promise of eternal life. On Calvary, when the good thief turned to Jesus with trust, he received the assurance of heaven: *"This day you will be with Me in paradise."*

Hope is not wishful thinking but confident trust in God's mercy. Even in our last hour, His love is greater than our sins.

Sheen on Hope in the Second Word

"One thief died in despair, the other in hope. Despair fixed its eyes on sin; hope fixed its eyes on the Savior. Hope does not deny the past but trusts in mercy stronger than sin."

Archbishop Sheen stressed that hope is always possible, no matter how dark the hour, because salvation rests not on our worthiness but on Christ's Cross.

Illustration – Conversion at the End

A man estranged from the Church for decades received the Sacraments on his deathbed. Whispering the prayer of the thief — *"Remember me, Lord"* — he died in peace. His story shows that hope is never too late, and that heaven is open to all who turn to Christ.

Invitation – Living Hope Daily

Hope is not only for the dying but for the living. It calls us to trust God's promises in our daily struggles — in sickness, in failure, in sin. To live with hope is to believe that every cross is the doorway to paradise.

Ask yourself:

- *Do I allow despair to cloud my view of God's mercy?*
- *Where do I need to place more trust in His promises?*
- *Am I living as one who believes in heaven?*

Closing Prayer

Lord Jesus, You gave hope to the thief on the Cross. Give me hope in every trial, trust in every failure, and confidence in Your mercy. Let my last breath echo his prayer: "Remember me, Lord, when You come into Your kingdom."

Amen.

Reflection 3:
Practicing the Virtue of Prudence

The Third Word: *"Behold your Mother."*

Reflection – The Wisdom of Love

Prudence is the virtue of choosing rightly, guided by truth and love. On Calvary, Jesus entrusted His Mother to John and John to His Mother. In this act, He revealed prudence at its highest — not self-preservation, but the wise care of souls.

Prudence sees beyond the moment. It considers God's will, the needs of others, and the eternal consequences of our choices.

Sheen on Prudence in the Third Word

"Prudence is not mere caution, but right reason in action. Our Lord, in His dying wisdom, provided for His Mother and His Church. He showed that prudence is love seeing far ahead, love preparing for the future."

Archbishop Sheen explained that true prudence is never selfish calculation, but the wise ordering of all things toward God.

Illustration – A Saint's Wise Choice

St. Maximilian Kolbe, in Auschwitz, offered his life in place of a condemned prisoner. His prudence was not worldly strategy but supernatural wisdom: recognizing that to save another's life was to fulfill God's will.

His act, like Christ's word to Mary and John, shows prudence as love expressed in wise sacrifice.

Invitation – Choosing in the Light of the Cross

To practice prudence is to let the Cross guide our decisions. It means asking not, *"What is easiest?"* but *"What is truest, holiest, most loving?"*

Ask yourself:

- *Do I make choices based on comfort or on God's will?*
- *Am I seeking the eternal good of others, as Jesus did for His Mother?*
- *How can I let prudence guide me in small daily decisions?*

Closing Prayer

Lord Jesus, in Your wisdom You gave us Your Mother. Teach me prudence in my choices, that I may seek what is true, choose what is holy, and act always in love. May my decisions reflect the wisdom of Calvary.

Amen.

Reflection 4:
Practicing the Virtue of Faith

The Fourth Word: *"My God, My God, why have You forsaken Me?"*

Reflection – Trust in Darkness

Faith is not proven when everything is clear, but when God seems silent. On the Cross, Jesus cried out the words of Psalm 22 — the prayer of the suffering just man. Though He felt the weight of abandonment, He entrusted Himself still to the Father.

Faith does not remove the darkness; it holds firm within it. At Calvary, Christ shows that to believe in the Father amid silence is the highest act of trust.

Sheen on Faith in the Fourth Word

"The greatest act of faith is to trust when there is no sign, no consolation, no answer. Our Lord's cry was not despair, but faith — faith clinging to the Father when the Father seemed absent."

Archbishop Sheen often said that true faith is forged in trial. Like Christ on the Cross, the believer says: *"I do not see, but I still believe."*

Illustration – The Dark Night of Faith

St. Teresa of Calcutta endured decades of spiritual dryness, often feeling abandoned by God. Yet she continued her mission with unwavering fidelity, loving the poorest of the poor. Her faith was not based on feelings, but on trust — the same faith Jesus lived on Calvary.

Invitation – Believing in the Silence

Faith calls us to trust when prayers seem unanswered, when trials press heavy, when God feels distant. To practice faith is to echo Jesus' cry, turning apparent absence into an offering of love.

Ask yourself:

- *Do I measure faith by feelings, or by fidelity?*
- *Am I willing to trust God even when He seems far away?*
- *How can I let my trials become acts of deeper faith?*

Closing Prayer

My God, when You seem far, teach me to believe. When I feel abandoned, let me cling to You in trust. May my faith be steady, not in consolations, but in Your Cross, where love endures even in silence.

Amen.

Reflection 5:
Practicing the Virtue of Temperance

The Fifth Word: *"I thirst."*

Reflection – Desire Ordered by Love

Temperance is the virtue that governs our desires, directing them toward what is truly good. On the Cross, Jesus spoke of thirst — not merely physical, but spiritual. He thirsted for souls, for love, for the fulfillment of the Father's will.

In Christ's cry, we learn that temperance is not the denial of desire, but its transformation. Our hearts find satisfaction only when their thirst is for God.

Sheen on Temperance in the Fifth Word

"When Our Lord said, 'I thirst,' He revealed the deepest longing of His Heart — for our love. Temperance is not the extinction of desire, but its sanctification. Our Lord's thirst teaches us to crave not the things of earth, but the things of heaven."

Archbishop Sheen taught that Christ purifies our desires, lifting them from selfish satisfaction to self-giving love.

Illustration – A Saint's Thirst

St. Augustine, who once sought pleasure in the world, found peace only in God. He prayed: *"You have made us for Yourself, O Lord, and our hearts are restless until they rest in You."* His conversion is a witness to temperance — desires ordered by grace toward eternal love.

Invitation – Purifying My Desires

Temperance is lived when we discipline our appetites, moderating what is good and rejecting what enslaves us. Above all, it is lived when our deepest thirst is for God's love.

Ask yourself:

- *What desires in my life need to be purified?*
- *Do I thirst more for the world's pleasures or for God's will?*
- *How can I let Christ redirect my desires to what truly satisfies?*

Closing Prayer

O Jesus, who thirsted for souls upon the Cross, purify my desires. Teach me to hunger and thirst for righteousness, to crave Your love above all else, and to order my life toward You. Let my thirst be joined to Yours, until it is quenched in eternity.

Amen.

Reflection 6:
Practicing the Virtue of Justice

The Sixth Word: *"It is finished."*

Reflection – Giving What Is Due

Justice is the virtue of rendering to God and to others what is rightfully theirs. On Calvary, Jesus declared: *"It is finished."* In that moment, He fulfilled justice perfectly — giving to the Father complete obedience, and to humanity complete redemption.

Justice is not merely about fairness but about fidelity: giving God our worship, our neighbor our love, and fulfilling our duties with integrity.

Sheen on Justice in the Sixth Word

"Justice was satisfied on the Cross, not by a balance of scales, but by the gift of a life. Our Lord paid the debt of sin, rendering to the Father perfect love and to mankind perfect mercy."

Archbishop Sheen explained that the Cross reveals justice not as cold law, but as love fulfilling every demand of truth.

Illustration – A Life Well Finished

St. Paul could say at the end of his life: *"I have fought the good fight, I have finished the race, I have kept the faith."* (2 Tim 4:7) His perseverance reflected Christ's justice — finishing the work entrusted to him, giving God and man what was due.

Invitation – Living Justice Daily

Justice is practiced when we fulfill our obligations: to God in prayer and worship, to others in honesty and charity, to ourselves in integrity. To live justly is to finish our tasks with faithfulness, however small.

Ask yourself:

- *Am I faithful in giving God His due through prayer and worship?*
- *Do I fulfill my duties toward others with honesty and charity?*
- *Am I living with the goal of finishing well, as Christ did?*

Closing Prayer

Lord Jesus, You finished the work of our redemption. Teach me to live justly: faithful to God, honest with others, true to my calling. Grant me perseverance to finish my race, and at the end, to hear You say: *"It is finished."*

Amen.

Reflection 7:
Practicing the Virtue of Charity

The Seventh Word: *"Father, into Your hands I commend My spirit."*

Reflection – Love Surrendered Completely

Charity is the greatest of the virtues, binding all the others together. On Calvary, Jesus' final word was one of surrender — giving Himself entirely into the Father's hands. In that act, His love was complete: for the Father, for humanity, for every soul He came to redeem.

Charity is not sentiment but self-giving. It is the willingness to place all we are and all we have into God's hands.

Sheen on Charity in the Seventh Word

"Charity is the soul of all virtue. Faith and hope will pass away, but charity will endure forever. On the Cross, charity reached its fullness as Our Lord surrendered His spirit to the Father for love of us."

Archbishop Sheen explained that the Cross is charity incarnate — love giving itself without limit, even unto death.

Illustration – A Saint's Final Offering

St. Thérèse of Lisieux, in her last moments, whispered: *"My God, I love You."* Her little way culminated in this final act of charity, surrendering her life into the hands of God with childlike trust.

Her death, like Christ's final word, shows that charity is the perfection of Christian life: to die in love, as we have lived in love.

Invitation – Living Charity as Surrender

To practice charity is to love God above all and neighbor as oneself. It means surrendering our will, our possessions, our time, our hearts into God's hands, confident that love is never lost in Him.

Ask yourself:

- *Am I willing to surrender everything into God's hands in love?*
- *How can I practice charity not only in words, but in daily sacrifices?*
- *Do I see charity as the crown of all virtues, the goal of my life?*

Closing Prayer

Father of Love, into Your hands I commend my spirit. Teach me to live in charity, to surrender my life as an offering of love, and to give myself without reserve, as Christ did upon the Cross. May charity crown my days, and be my final word at life's end. **Amen.**

Part III – Living the Beatitudes

Introduction

When Jesus first proclaimed the Beatitudes on the Mount, He described the way of life that leads to blessedness. On Calvary, He lived them all. Poverty of spirit, mercy, purity of heart, meekness, and even persecution — each found its fulfillment in the Crucified.

The Beatitudes are not soft ideals but heroic virtues, shining most brightly at the Cross. To live them is to embrace the paradox of Christian life: to find joy in sacrifice, strength in meekness, and eternal reward in seeming loss. These reflections invite us to walk with Christ from the Mount of the Beatitudes to the Hill of Calvary, and to let His blessings shape our lives.

- Reflection 1 – Blessed are the meek, for they shall inherit the earth
- Reflection 2 – Blessed are the merciful, for they shall obtain mercy
- Reflection 3 – Blessed are the pure in heart, for they shall see God
- Reflection 4 – Blessed are the poor in spirit, for theirs is the kingdom of heaven

- Reflection 5 – Blessed are those who hunger and thirst for justice, for they shall be satisfied
- Reflection 6 – Blessed are the peacemakers, for they shall be called children of God
- Reflection 7 – Blessed are those who mourn, for they shall be comforted
- Reflection 8 – Blessed are those who are persecuted for righteousness' sake, for theirs is the kingdom of heaven

Reflection 1:
Living the Beatitude: Blessed are the meek, for they shall inherit the earth.

The First Word: *"Father, forgive them, for they know not what they do."*

Reflection – Meekness as Strength Under Control

Meekness is not weakness. It is the strength of the soul under discipline, refusing to answer violence with violence. On Calvary, Jesus revealed meekness in perfection: in the midst of brutality and injustice, He responded not with wrath but with forgiveness.

Meekness disarms anger and calms hatred. It inherits the earth not by conquest but by mercy.

Sheen on Meekness in the First Word

"The world believes the strong man is the one who strikes back. Christ taught that the meek man is the one who can dominate himself. By forgiving, He conquered anger; by being silent, He conquered pride."

Archbishop Sheen explained that meekness does not destroy justice but fulfills it through mercy.

Illustration – The Strength of Meekness

Mahatma Gandhi once remarked that the Sermon on the Mount was the greatest sermon on nonviolence. Yet it is on Calvary, in Jesus' meek forgiveness, that its truth is revealed most fully. Christian meekness is not passive but active love, turning enemies into brothers.

Invitation – Practicing Meekness in My Life

Meekness is lived in our homes, our workplaces, and our parishes when we choose patience over harshness, forgiveness over retaliation, gentleness over cruelty.

Ask yourself:

- *Do I lash out when wronged, or do I seek meekness in response?*
- *Am I willing to let go of vengeance for the sake of peace?*
- *How can I imitate Christ's meekness in daily conflicts?*

Closing Prayer

Lord Jesus, meek and humble of heart, You forgave those who crucified You. Teach me to be meek, to master my anger, and to conquer hatred with love. Grant that I may inherit the peace of Your kingdom, not by force, but by mercy.

Amen.

Reflection 2:
Living the Beatitude: Blessed are the merciful, for they shall obtain mercy.

The Second Word: *"This day you will be with Me in Paradise."*

Reflection – Mercy in the Face of Sin

Mercy is love bending down to lift misery. On Calvary, the good thief confessed his guilt and asked only to be remembered. Jesus answered with mercy far greater than he hoped: *"This day you will be with Me in Paradise."*

Mercy does not excuse sin, but heals it. It looks at misery with compassion, not scorn, and opens heaven where there was only despair.

Sheen on Mercy in the Second Word

"The thief had nothing to recommend him — no good works, no defense, no future. But he had one thing: faith in mercy. And mercy did not disappoint. Mercy is love answering sin with forgiveness."

Archbishop Sheen stressed that mercy is not weakness but the very strength of God's love poured out upon the unworthy.

Illustration – Mercy at the Last Hour

A priest once told of being called to the bedside of a hardened sinner. With tears, the man whispered, *"Father, forgive me."* He died shortly after receiving absolution. Like the good thief, he entered eternity clinging to mercy alone.

Invitation – Practicing Mercy Daily

Mercy is not only for God to give, but for us to share. To practice mercy is to forgive others, to comfort the sorrowful, to bear wrongs patiently, and to remember that as we give, so we shall receive.

Ask yourself:

- *Do I withhold mercy from those who wrong me?*
- *Am I quick to judge, or quick to forgive?*
- *How can I show mercy in concrete ways to those around me?*

Closing Prayer

Lord Jesus, You showed mercy to the thief on the Cross. Show mercy also to me in my weakness. Help me to forgive as I have been forgiven, to love as I have been loved, and to obtain mercy by practicing mercy.

Amen.

Reflection 3:
Living the Beatitude: Blessed are the pure in heart, for they shall see God.

The Third Word: *"Behold your Mother."*

Reflection – Purity as Undivided Love

Purity of heart is not merely freedom from lust but freedom from all duplicity, all self-seeking. At Calvary, Jesus gave His Mother to John, and John to His Mother — a bond of love undefiled, a new family born from the Cross.

Purity means to see others as God sees them — as gifts, not objects; as persons, not possessions. To be pure in heart is to live with undivided love.

Sheen on Purity in the Third Word

"Purity is not the absence of passion but the re-direction of it. The impure heart sees flesh; the pure heart sees souls. On the Cross, Our Lord lifted love to its highest by giving us His Mother."

Archbishop Sheen emphasized that purity of heart enables us to see God not only in heaven, but here on earth, in His image reflected in others.

Illustration – A Life of Pure Devotion

St. Maria Goretti, a young martyr for chastity, forgave her attacker as she lay dying. Her heart, pure and undivided, saw God even in her moment of trial. Her life remains a testament to the Beatitude of purity.

Invitation – Seeking Purity of Heart

Purity of heart demands vigilance, prayer, and sacrifice. But it is also a gift — the grace to see with clear eyes, to love without selfishness, and to live with a heart set on God.

Ask yourself:

- *Do I seek to see others with pure eyes and love them as God's children?*
- *Are there attachments or sins clouding my heart's vision?*
- *Am I asking daily for the grace to live with a clean heart?*

Closing Prayer

Lord Jesus, You gave us Your Mother from the Cross. Through her intercession, create in me a clean heart. Help me to see You in others, to love without selfishness, and to live with a heart undivided.

Amen.

Reflection 4
Living the Beatitude:
Blessed are the poor in spirit, for theirs is the kingdom of heaven.

The Fourth Word: *"My God, My God, why have You forsaken Me?"*

Reflection – Poverty of Spirit as Dependence on God

To be poor in spirit is to recognize our utter need for God. On Calvary, Jesus entered into the deepest poverty: stripped of comfort, abandoned by friends, and even feeling the silence of the Father. Yet in this poverty, He clung to faith, entrusting Himself completely to God.

Poverty of spirit is not misery, but freedom — freedom from self-reliance, freedom to trust God in everything.

Sheen on Poverty of Spirit in the Fourth Word

"The cry of abandonment was not despair, but the prayer of the poor in spirit. Christ, bereft of every comfort, clung still to the Father. The poor in spirit are those who, having nothing, possess everything in God."

Archbishop Sheen explained that the kingdom belongs to the poor in spirit because they rely entirely on the King.

Illustration – Faith in the Midst of Loss

A widow who lost her husband and children in war said, *"I have nothing left – but I still have God."* Her poverty of spirit did not destroy her but made her a living witness of faith in God's sufficiency.

Invitation – Choosing Poverty of Spirit

To live this Beatitude is to hold earthly goods lightly and to seek our true security in God alone. It is to say with Christ, even in desolation: *"My God."*

Ask yourself:

- *Do I cling to possessions, achievements, or control for security?*
- *Am I willing to let God be enough, even when everything else fails?*
- *How can I practice poverty of spirit in daily life?*

Closing Prayer

My God, when I feel abandoned, teach me to trust You. Grant me the poverty of spirit that clings to You alone. May I find my treasure not in possessions, but in Your kingdom.

Amen.

Reflection 5:
Living the Beatitude: Blessed are those who hunger and thirst for justice, for they shall be satisfied.

The Fifth Word: *"I thirst."*

Reflection – Holy Desire that Satisfies

Jesus' cry of thirst was not only for water but for righteousness, for souls, for the fulfillment of the Father's will. This Beatitude calls us to cultivate holy desires, to thirst not for fleeting pleasures but for justice, truth, and holiness.

Those who hunger and thirst for justice are never left empty — for their desire aligns with God's own Heart.

Sheen on Holy Desire in the Fifth Word

"The world is full of thirsts which never satisfy — the thirst for pleasure, for power, for wealth. But only one thirst satisfies: the thirst for justice, which is the thirst for God Himself."

Archbishop Sheen taught that to hunger for justice is to direct our desires to their highest fulfillment — in Christ, who alone satisfies.

Illustration – A Saint's Burning Thirst

St. Catherine of Siena once prayed: *"My Lord, I hunger for souls."* Her holy thirst drove her to serve the poor, reform the Church, and counsel popes. Her life was a testimony that to thirst for God's justice is to be filled with His strength.

Invitation – Purifying My Desires

To live this Beatitude is to examine what we hunger for. Earthly desires leave us empty, but the thirst for holiness, truth, and love fills us with God.

Ask yourself:

- *What do I thirst for most deeply?*
- *Are my desires ordered toward God or toward myself?*
- *How can I redirect my hunger to seek holiness above all?*

Closing Prayer

O Jesus, who thirsted for souls upon the Cross, give me a thirst for holiness. Satisfy my hunger with Your justice, and fill me with the joy that comes only from You.

Amen.

Reflection 6:
Living the Beatitude:
Blessed are the peacemakers, for they shall be called children of God.

The Sixth Word: *"It is finished."*

Reflection – Peace Through Completion

Peace is not the absence of conflict but the presence of wholeness. On Calvary, Jesus declared: *"It is finished."* He completed the work of redemption, reconciling heaven and earth. In that moment, true peace was made: the peace of the Cross.

Peacemakers are those who bring reconciliation — not by avoiding sacrifice, but by finishing the work of love, even when it costs.

Sheen on Peacemaking in the Sixth Word

"Peace is the tranquility of order. On the Cross, Christ put all things in order by doing the Father's will to the end. The greatest peacemakers are those who bring others into harmony with God."

Archbishop Sheen taught that peace cannot be built on compromise with sin, but only on truth lived to completion.

Illustration – A Bridge of Peace

St. Francis of Assisi once went unarmed into the camp of the Muslim sultan during the Crusades, risking death to proclaim Christ. Though they disagreed, the sultan honored him as a man of peace. Francis' courage showed that peacemaking is not cowardice but the fruit of fidelity.

Invitation – Becoming a Peacemaker

To live this Beatitude is to finish the tasks of love, to build bridges of reconciliation, and to bear the cost of peace.

Ask yourself:

- *Do I avoid conflict at the expense of truth?*
- *Am I willing to pay the price of bringing peace where there is division?*
- *How can I finish the work of love in my family, parish, or community?*

Closing Prayer

Lord Jesus, You finished the work of redemption and brought peace to the world. Make me a peacemaker, willing to bear the cost of reconciliation. Let me be called a child of God by sowing peace in Your name.

Amen.

Reflection 7:
Living the Beatitude:
Blessed are those who mourn, for they shall be comforted.

The Seventh Word: *"Father, into Your hands I commend My spirit."*

Reflection – Mourning Transformed by Trust

Mourning is the cry of the heart over loss, sin, and suffering. On Calvary, Jesus entered into the deepest sorrow as He surrendered His life into the Father's hands. Yet even in that final breath, sorrow was not despair but trust.

The Beatitude promises comfort to those who mourn because God Himself enters into their grief, turning tears into seeds of hope.

Sheen on Mourning in the Seventh Word

"Sorrow without faith leads to despair; sorrow with faith leads to comfort. Christ sanctified mourning by His own death, showing that tears can be pearls when placed in the hands of the Father."

Archbishop Sheen explained that Christian mourning is not hopelessness, but the path to consolation in God.

Illustration – Tears that Became Prayer

A mother wept for years over her son who had abandoned the faith. At last, he returned to the sacraments before dying. Her mourning was turned to consolation, echoing the words of Scripture: *"Those who sow in tears shall reap rejoicing."* (Ps. 126:5)

Invitation – Mourning with Hope

To live this Beatitude is to bring our griefs, our sins, and our losses into God's hands. He alone can transform mourning into comfort.

Ask yourself:

- *Do I allow sorrow to lead me to God, or do I let it turn to despair?*
- *What grief do I need to place into the Father's hands?*
- *Can I trust that He will bring comfort even from my tears?*

Closing Prayer

Father of Consolation, into Your hands I commend my spirit. Take my sorrows and transform them, my tears and sanctify them, my mourning and comfort it with Your love.

Amen.

Reflection 8:
Living the Beatitude:
Blessed are those who are persecuted for righteousness' sake, for theirs is the kingdom of heaven.

"And bowing His head, He gave up His spirit."

Reflection – Persecution Embraced in Love

Persecution comes when the world resists truth. On Calvary, Jesus was persecuted not for wrongdoing, but for righteousness — for being the Truth itself. His last breath sanctified every sacrifice made by those who suffer for His name.

The Beatitude promises that persecution is not defeat, but a share in Christ's victory. The kingdom belongs to those who, like Him, remain faithful unto death.

Sheen on Persecution in the Final Word

"The world may tolerate a watered-down gospel, but it will always crucify righteousness. Our Lord's last breath was His triumph over persecution, for it proved that death could not conquer truth."

Archbishop Sheen often reminded Christians that fidelity will draw opposition, but the Cross transforms suffering into glory.

Illustration – Witness in Martyrdom

The early martyrs of Rome faced brutal deaths for refusing to deny Christ. As they perished, they sang hymns of joy. Their persecutors thought them defeated, but the blood of the martyrs became the seed of the Church.

Invitation – Faithful in Trial

To live this Beatitude is to accept that following Christ will bring opposition, yet to remain steadfast with love.

Ask yourself:

- *Am I willing to suffer ridicule or rejection for my faith?*
- *Do I compromise truth to avoid persecution?*
- *How can I stand firm in righteousness with love, not bitterness?*

Closing Prayer

Lord Jesus, You were persecuted unto death, Yet you triumphed in love. Strengthen me when I face opposition, make me steadfast in righteousness, and grant me courage to share in Your Cross, that I too may inherit the kingdom of heaven.

Amen.

Epilogue:
The Cross and the Christian Way of Life

The Cross does not leave us where it finds us. It frees us from the slavery of sin, strengthens us to practice virtue, and blesses us with the joy of the Beatitudes. Every step we take in overcoming anger, envy, lust, pride, gluttony, sloth, or greed; every effort to live faith, hope, charity, prudence, justice, temperance, and fortitude; every attempt to embody the spirit of the Beatitudes — all of it is a share in the victory of Calvary.

Archbishop Fulton Sheen often reminded us that holiness is not an idea but a way of life. The Cross is not only a mystery to be adored, it is a pattern to be lived. To overcome sin, to grow in virtue, to live the Beatitudes — this is to let the Crucified live in us.

May these reflections lead you not only to the foot of the Cross, but into a life shaped by it. And may you discover, as countless saints before you, that the Cross embraced with love is the surest path to joy, peace, and eternal glory.

Concluding Word: Sent from Calvary

You have walked through these pages as through a retreat — listening at Calvary, kneeling at the foot of the Cross, and hearing once again the Seven Last Words of Our Lord. Along the way, you have stood with the Blessed Mother, Mary and St. John, prayed with the saints, and discovered how the mystery of the Cross touches every part of life: our sufferings, our joys, our families, our vocations, our sins, our virtues, and our hopes.

The Cross is not only a moment in history; it is the pattern of discipleship. Every nail and thorn tells us of love. Every word spoken from the wood of the cross is spoken to you personally. The same Jesus who cried "I thirst" still thirsts for your love today; the same Lord who entrusted His Spirit to the Father now invites you to place your whole life into those same hands.

Do not be afraid to return often to Calvary. Make it the place of your prayer, the measure of your love, and the strength of your mission. In the

Cross you will find healing for wounds, pardon for sins, and hope for eternal life. In the Cross, you will also discover your own calling — to live, suffer, forgive, and rejoice with Christ until He comes again in glory.

As Archbishop Fulton Sheen reminded us: *"Unless there is a Good Friday in your life, there will never be an Easter Sunday."* May this book be not only a companion for meditation but a seed of transformation. May you leave these pages renewed in faith, strengthened in hope, and on fire with love.

About the Author

Allan Smith is a Catholic evangelist, radio host, and spiritual director who has spent over a decade proclaiming the wisdom of Archbishop Fulton J. Sheen to audiences around the world. As the founder of Bishop Sheen Today, he has edited and published dozens of classic Sheen titles, including 'The Cries of Jesus from the Cross' and 'Lord, Teach Us to Pray'.

A passionate promoter of Eucharistic Reparation and devotion to the Holy Face of Jesus, Allan regularly speaks at parish missions, leads retreats, and hosts weekly radio broadcasts across Canada, the United States, Ireland, Australia and the Philippines. His work has helped reintroduce Sheen's powerful spiritual legacy to a new generation.

He lives in Canada with his family and continues his mission of calling souls to deeper intimacy with Christ through the example of saints like St. Thérèse of Lisieux and the timeless teachings of Fulton Sheen.

To learn more or to access free devotional resources, visit our two websites at:

www.bishopsheentoday.com

www.holyfacemiracle.com

About the Sheen Mission Series

The Sheen Mission Series is a four-volume spiritual journey inspired by Archbishop Fulton J. Sheen. Each book is designed as a devotional companion — guiding the faithful in prayer, reparation, and renewal through the Holy Face of Jesus, the Cross, the Eucharist, and the maternal love of Our Blessed Mother.

The series can be read in any order, yet together it forms a complete mission of grace:

- **Volume I –** *The Holy Face and the Little Way*
  Walk with St. Thérèse of Lisieux in her Little Way of love, united to the devotion of the Holy Face of Jesus.

- **Volume II –** *Behold Your Mother*
  Enter into Mary's tender care at the foot of the Cross and discover the strength of her Seven Sorrows.

- **Volume III – *The Cross and the Last Words*** Pray with Archbishop Sheen at Calvary as he opens the treasures of the Seven Last Words of Christ.

- **Volume IV – *Lord, Show Us Thy Face and We Shall Be Saved***

    A mission of light and transformation, centered on the Eucharist and the saving power of Christ's Face.

The Sheen Mission Series invites you to walk with Archbishop Fulton J. Sheen in prayer, reparation, and renewal — a journey of the Holy Face, the Cross, the Eucharist, and Our Blessed Mother.

J M J

A Personal Invitation

Over the years, I have had the privilege of helping souls draw closer to Christ through prayer, silence, and the beautiful wisdom of Archbishop Fulton J. Sheen.

If this devotional has nourished your heart, you may also find these works helpful in your journey of faith:

Advent and Christmas with Archbishop Fulton J. Sheen

- A Devotional Journey of Waiting, Welcoming, and Living the Mystery

Daily readings and gentle reflections to guide the heart from hope to joy — from the quiet longing of Advent to the radiant wonder of Christmas.

Priest, Prophet & King

- Meditations on Identity, Mission, and the Call to Holiness

Reflections on what it means to truly belong to Christ — in our families, vocations, and daily life.

The Sheen Mission Series
Collected Meditations

- Over 100 of the Richest Reflections from Retreats, Radio, and Prayer

A treasury to keep on the nightstand — for those ten-minute moments of quiet that become encounters with God.

May every book you read be an open door to the heart of Christ.

May these works draw you deeper into prayer, trust, peace, and surrender.

And may the Child of Bethlehem be born again in you.

Come, Lord Jesus.

To learn more or to stay connected:
www.bishopsheentoday.com

Archbishop Fulton J. Sheen

† *Ora pro nobis* †

www.ingramcontent.com/pod-product-compliance
Lightning Source LLC
Chambersburg PA
CBHW070638050426
42451CB00008B/204